Just Whit,
I love you
tons and I'm my
even glad you're my
"little sister"! Merry
Christmas!
Love,
Bicky
Christmas 1984

The Snarkout Boys & The Baconburg Horror

The Snarkout Boys & The Baconburg Horror

by Daniel Pinkwater

LOTHROP, LEE & SHEPARD BOOKS

NEW YORK

1   2   3   4   5   6   7   8   9   10
Library of Congress Cataloging in Publication Data
Pinkwater, Daniel Manus, (date)
The snarkout boys and the Baconburg horror.
Summary: Walter Galt, Winston Bongo, and their female
friend Rat have an adventure involving a beatnik poet
and a werewolf.
[1. Humorous stories] I. Title.
PZ7.P6335Snar   1984   83-19544
ISBN 0-688-02670-2
Design by Camilla Filancia

Once again, it is my pleasure and my obligation

to offer this little book to my friend Ken Kelman

The moon rises. The leaves tremble in the night wind. Dark covers the city. I wait in my place of hiding.

I am changing. I feel my bones and sinews shift and move in the first light of the full moon. My nose gets longer. My skin tingles as fur sprouts everywhere. I become aware of a thousand things unseen and unheard by humans. I smell things. I feel things on the tips of my hairs. In parks and cemeteries and vacant lots, rat and raccoon, cat and opossum—the little children of the night—begin to stir. Now and then they catch a scent of me on the breeze and shiver in their skins.

My teeth are fangs now. My nails have turned hard and horny, and black and sharp. Far beneath me, the city turns to slumber. I crouch beneath the water tank, high atop the city's tallest building. Faintly, I hear my little brothers, the zoo wolves, raise their voices in greeting to the enormous autumn moon.

Few creatures, and fewer humans, dream that I exist—and those who know me, know me only as a frightened dream, an imagined flitting dark moment. I am invisible. My cunning and instinct protect me from the sight of men—but I will move among them. I will lurk beneath their windows, race their cars on darkened streets, lope through the open places, and climb the high buildings.

The moon is well into the sky now. The lights in

the houses are going out. It is almost time for me to begin my running. I tear my civics textbook in two. The binding makes a satisfying snapping sound. I distribute the pages into the night air. They flutter toward earth.

Now I am ready to scamper down the exterior of the tall building, to run, to cavort, perhaps to terrify those with the wit to see—or almost see—to sense my nearness.

I rise up on my haunches and announce myself to the night. I give the ancient cry—the howl of the wolf-man.

For more than a year, my friend Winston Bongo and I have been snarking out together.

Snarking is the art of sneaking out of the house when your parents are sleeping, and having an adventure late at night. The adventure usually includes or consists of going to the movies at the Snark Theater, from which the art of Snarking takes its name. The Snark is open all night 365 days a year, and it has a different double bill every twenty-four hours.

Winston and I began snarking together in our first week of high school, and kept it up all through our freshman year. In the summer we snarked out nightly. As we entered our second year of high school, we had both become highly expert world-class snarkers.

There's a box in the lobby of the Snark into which you can put a slip of paper with the name of any movie ever made, and the Snark will try to get the movie and show it. They usually get it—and they will send you a free pass to see the movie—if the one you've requested is one they've never shown before. Theoretically, someone who knows a lot about movies could go to the Snark free any number of times. If you write your birthday on a slip of paper and put it in the box, the Snark will send you a free pass on your birthday too.

It's more than a movie house. It's a way of life.

It costs fifty cents to get in if you have identification showing that you are a college student. Our I.D.'s are fakes. Nobody really cares.

We're not the only kids in town who snark out. When you snark regularly, you begin to recognize some faces around the soda machine and develop a nodding acquaintance with some unusual people. You don't get into friendships with other snarkers very quickly. Many people who snark are introverts—quiet types. You may run into someone fifty times before you have a conversation of a dozen words.

Winston and I have one friend we meet at the Snark—a girl named Rat. Her real name is Bentley Saunders Harrison Matthews. We call her Rat. So does her family. She likes the name.

Rat doesn't snark out with us—that is, she doesn't make a date to meet on a street corner and go down to the Snark the way Winston and I do. She's more of an independent solo snarker.

"If I'm there, I'm there," Rat says. When Rat turns up at the Snark, we find her sitting in an aisle seat, hunched down, her legs twisted around each other, chewing her knuckles. Draped over two seats next to her will be her oversized red jacket, which she says is just like a jacket James Dean had. Without taking her eyes off the screen, Rat will punch one of us in the hip with a bony knuckle as we move down the aisle, and motion us to the two saved seats.

The movie could be anything—*Sabu the Elephant Boy*, Doris Day, or *The Cabinet of Dr. Caligari*—Rat doesn't miss a single second. I don't think she even blinks. If you talk during the movie she'll give you a sharp poke. This applies to strangers nearby as well as to Winston and me.

Rat is skinny and wiry. When she hits you it hurts. There are some not-so-nice characters who go to the

Snark and try to creep on people, boys as well as girls. Rat just gives them a rap when they start with her, and the creepers change their seats. The fact is, Rat is tougher than us, and we both know it. So does she.

I can count on the fingers of one hand the number of times Rat has spoken while the film is running. Therefore it was noteworthy when she spoke to us during a movie with Laird Cregar, one of her favorite actors. What she said was also unprecedented: "If you guys are willing to skip the second feature, I'd like you to come with me. There's something I want to show you."

Missing the second feature was no sacrifice. It had Charlton Heston in it. Almost all the movies on Winston's list of the worst movies in history have Charlton Heston—or Jeff Chandler. If Rat had not been present, we would have enjoyed the film by making obscene remarks about the actors and talking back to the screen, like the rest of the audience. However, with our friend present, we would have had no choice but to sit through it, silently suffering.

When the Laird Cregar movie was over, we followed Rat up the aisle and out of the movie house. "I think you'll be interested in this place I found," she said.

Rat led us through dark streets for a number of blocks. We were in a run-down and scuzzy part of town a little to the north of the Snark. It was an area Winston and I did not know well.

We went down a street which had a partially bombed-out appearance. Most of the stores were boarded up, and there were lights in only a few of the buildings above the store fronts. We stopped in front of a store that looked deserted at first, it was so dark inside. Then we saw candles burning through the plate glass windows, and we smelled something spicy, like cinnamon. Lettered on the window of the store were the words DHARMA BUNS COFFEE HOUSE.

"This is it," Rat said.

"This is what?" I asked.

"It's a coffee house," Rat said. "It's been here for years. There used to be all sorts of stuff like this aroundhere—andbeatniks—myuncletoldmeaboutit."

Rat's uncle, Flipping Hades Terwilliger, was someone we knew fairly well. Winston and I had helped find him once when he was kidnapped, and on other occasions had searched for him when he was merely lost. Uncle Flipping is the sort of person apt to get lost and kidnapped. If they ever have organized competitions for the weird, Uncle Flipping is my pick for World's Heavyweight Champion.

"So? What's so good about this?" Winston asked.

"Idiot! Poets hang out here," Rat said impatiently.

"Big deal," Winston said. "What I want to know is, have you been here before? I mean, does it cost much to get in? I don't want to spend a lot of money."

"Well, you just sort of go in, and you order coffee, and you sit around, and all the great artists and poets and people like that are there—and it's just a neat place, that's all," Rat said.

I had the impression that she'd never been inside this Dharma Buns Coffee House. What was more, she was a little nervous about going in alone, and that was why she wanted us with her. This was not in keeping with her character as it was expressed around the Snark Theater.

"So, do you want to go in or what?" Winston asked.

"Makes no difference to me," Rat said.

She wanted to go into the coffee house, all right, and Winston knew it. He was just enjoying the unusual spectacle of Rat at a disadvantage.

"Who knows how much they charge in there?" Winston said. "A cup of coffee probably costs two dollars. I've only got a little more than two dollars, and I expect to snark out twice more this week. I'm not sure I want to go into any expensive clip joint."

"Look, it will be my treat, all right?" Rat hissed. "Now do you want to go in or not?"

"I never say no to a free drink," Winston said, "but are you sure you wouldn't rather go to the Hasty Tasty?"

The Hasty Tasty was an extra-greasy spoon across the street from the Snark. It was where we'd usually go for a root beer or a stale doughnut.

Rat glared.

"If we go in, are you going to get us something to eat too?" Winston asked Rat. "It smells like they have pastry or cinnamon buns or something."

He was pushing it. I took pity on Rat, and probably also saved Winston from getting a lump on the head. "Let's go in already," I said. "I'm tired of standing around in the street."

We went from the darkness of the street into the darker darkness of the Dharma Buns Coffee House and an utterly different world.

It took a little while to get used to the darkness inside the Dharma Buns Coffee House. We sort of felt our way to a table made from one of those giant wooden spools they use for electric cable. There were some rickety chairs around the table. We sat down.

The only light in the place came from a candle on each table. The candles were stuck in old wine bottles with drippings of colored wax down the sides. The walls were hung with paintings, stuffed animal heads, signs, busted musical instruments, a suit of armor, and all kinds of junk.

At the other tables was an assortment of strange people. Most of the men had beards or big moustaches, and the women had on clothing which looked as though it had been made from tableclothes and bedspreads. There were a lot of sandals in evidence.

A stereo was playing loud jazz. Some people were playing chess. There was a lot of talking going on.

It was a much more interesting place than the Hasty Tasty. I was glad we had come, even if coffee did cost two dollars.

A waitress came over. She was dressed all in black, and had pale, almost white makeup all over her face—even her lips.

"Can I get you anything?" the waitress asked.

Winston likes to appear sophisticated. He leaned back in his chair and asked, "What have you got?"

"Coffee," said the waitress, "and cinnamon buns."

She didn't so much say the words as breathe them. It sounded tragic, as though she were saying "death" instead of coffee, and "disaster" instead of cinnamon buns.

"We'll have three coffees," Rat said.

"Three coffees," the waitress said, as if she were saying "the end of mankind." She went to get the coffee.

"Is she weird!" Winston said.

"Shut up," Rat said.

The jazz record finished, and this guy got up to sing. He had a guitar. Someone had switched on a spotlight. The singer sat on a stool, in the light of the spot. Nobody introduced him. He sang the longest and most boring song I'd ever heard. It was about a maritime disaster on the Great Lakes. The song told about the wreck of a freighter called the *Hortense Matilda McAllister* in 1957. All five crew members got wet—nobody drowned—because the boat sank at the dock in Toledo, Ohio. The singer had a lot of trouble with rhymes because of the name of the boat. There were about sixty stanzas, all more or less the same. The guitar playing was diabolical. The crowd seemed to like it—at least they listened attentively.

During the song the waitress came by with our coffees. "Six dollars," she said the way you'd tell someone that his best friend had died. Rat shelled out.

In my opinion the coffee at the Hasty Tasty was better. Winston said that probably the coffee in hell was better. Rat told us to be quiet—she was listening to the song.

As I feared, the folksinger did an encore. It was a sort of sad love ballad. I can't describe it other than to say that I'd rather be shot through the head than listen to it again. Rat liked it even better than the first song. Winston was sorry we hadn't stayed and watched Charlton Heston.

Rat was getting annoyed. Obviously she liked the Dharma Buns Coffee House and everything about it. She was close to socking Winston in the head, but she hadn't done so yet because we were in a classy grown-up place, and she didn't want to appear to be nothing but an insignificant high school sophomore.

Things began to look up. The folksinger left. He was replaced by a poet named Jonathan Quicksilver. He launched right into a poem.

```
                           THE STOP LIGHT ON THE CORNER

                                OF FIFTH AND SNARK

    IS WHANGING

            BANGING

               CLANGING IN THE WIND

    OH JAMES DEAN      WHERE ARE YOU      NOW

                            SQUASHED

                            IN

                            YOUR

                            PORSCHE

                                 JUST WHEN WE NEED

                                         YOU

       AND

    THE MUSCLEBOUND CRUM-BUMS

                           THREATEN TO BEAT ME UP

              JUST

              CAUSE

              I'M

              WEIRD

                            *
```

It was better than the folk song. For one thing, it was a lot shorter. Also, Quicksilver had no guitar. I was sort of impressed. I had never seen a poet before. He did some more poems.

```
                         HOPALONG CASSIDY

                              YOU USED TO BE A BIG DEAL
       YOU        AND YOUR HORSE

                              TONY             EVERYBODY
   LOVED    YOU           THEN THEY FORGOT ABOUT YOU

                         AND IF THEY REMEMBERED YOU

                         THEY REMEMBERED YOU AS A PUNK

                         COWBOY ACTOR IN A BLACK SUIT

                                   BUT I NEVER FORGOT YOU

                                   HOPALONG

                         AND I GOT A BLACK SUIT TOO


                         AND IF I HAD A HORSE I'D CALL HIM

                         TONY

                         NO

                         THAT WAS SOME OTHER COWBOY'S HORSE
       WELL

                         YOU KNOW WHAT I MEAN

                                             RIGHT?

                              *
```

```
                        I'M REAL SENSITIVE

    I MEAN

                        I FEEL THINGS

                        BUT DOES ANYBODY NOTICE?

DO THOSE CHICKS NOTICE?

                        AND ARE THEY NICE TO ME?

                        HA!

                            THEY THINK I'M SOME KIND

OF CREEP

                    WHEN I'M DEAD

                            AND MY POEMS ARE FAMOUS

    THEY'LL BE SORRY

                        THEY'LL WISH THEY WERE A LOT NICER TO ME


BUT IT WILL BE TOO LATE

                THEN

                              *
```

Rat had come completely unglued. It so happened that she loved James Dean and had long since decided to dedicate her life to his memory—so when Quicksilver read that first poem in which he was mentioned, Rat decided that Quicksilver was great. The poem had also alluded to James Dean's death, an event she could hardly stand to think about—so she was in an emotional state—and when Quicksilver came over to our table to sell us an autographed book of poems, Rat handed over $6.95 without a second's hesitation.

Quicksilver also accepted a cup of coffee, which Winston offered, and Rat paid for. This evening of culture was costing her plenty, but she didn't seem to care that she was going through money like a fiend. She was really happy to be talking to a live poet.

She was also impressed with Quicksilver's appearance, which was singular. He was the littlest, scrawniest, palest guy possible. He was dressed all in black, and he had a big black cowboy hat, and carried a thick notebook. I supposed he had his newest poems in it. He had one of the biggest schnozzolas I'd ever seen— with freckles. His honker was as big as his head, almost. He was an admirable guy. I have to say it.

Rat's eyeglasses were shining in the candlelight. She was really taken with Quicksilver. For the first time in the more than a year I'd known her, I didn't have the vague feeling she might slug somebody at any moment.

Quicksilver sat around with us for a while and told us how jealous the other poets were of his work and lifestyle. I found out that he worked days in a Ms. Doughnut—that's a chain of roadside stands the trademark of which is this girl doughnut. They make them fresh, but they taste stale—I've never been able to understand it. Quicksilver told us they had a secret formula.

There was a scream from the kitchen. The waitress, the one in black with the white face, came out. She was hollering that something huge and dark and fast-moving had whisked through and frightened her.

"Sounds like a werewolf to me," Quicksilver said, "I'm going."

He was gone in two seconds. So was everybody else in the place. There was nothing for us to do but get up and go home—so we did.

Winston Bongo and Walter Galt attended Genghis Khan High School. Rat was a student at George Armstrong Custer High School. Therefore the three snarkers did not have the opportunity to see one another every day and discuss, among other things, the events of the night before. Some days might pass before they would meet.

Each night's adventure would end in the same way—Rat would abruptly leave the two boys on a street corner. Rarely would she allow them to walk her home. Rat liked to think over the movies she had seen as she walked. If Walter and Winston were with her she would have had to talk.

On the night the three had visited the Dharma Buns Coffee House, when the place suddenly emptied and the snark artists had wandered out into the street, Rat was not inclined to hear a single word from her friends. The experience of sitting in the coffee house, and what she thought about it, were things she wanted to keep to herself for the moment. "I'm going," she said, and was gone. Walter and Winston were used to this kind of leave-taking, and waved and grunted, which was all there was time for. Rat was across the street and around the corner, leaving the boys to find their own way out of the neighborhood.

Rat had a lot to think about on her way home. What she thought about was the way it had been in the Dharma Buns Coffee House, the feel of the warm mug in her hand, the darkness, the people sitting at the tables, and the poetry. It was the poetry she wanted to think about most. This was entirely different from the stuff in the literature book—as she had hoped it would be. This was not like the poetry Mrs. Starkley, the English teacher, made the class read:

St. Agnes' Eve—Ah, bitter chill it was!
The owl, for all his feathers, was a-cold;
The hare limp'd trembling through the frozen grass,
And silent was the flock in wooly fold—

Rat didn't actively dislike that sort of thing, but she didn't like it very much either. Mrs. Starkley made sure that Rat and the others would not actually enjoy poems. The impression Rat had was that Mrs. Starkley wanted to make sure her students showed the proper respect for poetry—but they were not supposed to like it. This was Rat's impression. She did not know for sure that Mrs. Starkley hated poetry.

Mrs. Starkley hated poetry. What Mrs. Starkley did not hate—but, in fact, loved—was Tuesday night wrestling on cable TV. She was a big fan. Her favorite wrestler was the Mighty Gorilla. The Mighty Gorilla was the uncle of Winston Bongo.

Mrs. Starkley never suspected that one of her students, Rat, was friends with Winston Bongo, the nephew of the wrestler she, Mrs. Starkley, most admired, and that she, Rat, had often eaten meals with him (The Mighty Gorilla). If Mrs. Starkley had known this, she would have thought about it quite a bit. Mrs. Starkley had a color picture of the Mighty Gorilla which she had cut out of a magazine. The color picture was taped to the door of the refrigerator. Mr. Starkley, Mrs. Starkley's husband, said that it, the picture, ruined his appetite. Mrs. Starkley said that would do him good, fat as he was. Mr. Starkley was not even as fat as the Mighty Gorilla.

Rat was not thinking about any of this. She did not even know that Mrs. Starkley was a wrestling fan. Rat was thinking about the poems of Jonathan Quicksilver. She was carrying the thin book that contained every poem he had ever written. The first thing Rat was going to do when she got home was read every one of those poems.

When she reached her street, the windows of all the houses were dark. The only illumination came from the streetlights. Rat's house was an old and big one, set back from the street behind an iron fence that was overgrown with vines. As she reached the gate, she thought she saw a large shadow flit before her. She was startled—and then decided it had only been a bat interrupting the light from the streetlamp in front of her house. She also felt a cold chill, and had the momentary sensation of being watched by someone or something crouching in the shrubbery.

Rat was not easily frightened. The werewolf scare at the Dharma Buns Coffee House had meant nothing to her. She was unfrightened now. She let herself into the darkened house without making a sound.

A pair of eyes watched from the bushes.

I ran, I loped through night streets. I jumped over cars. I smelled something. Coffee. Cinnamon. I went to investigate. A kitchen. A girl dressed in black. She screamed. I liked it. The others left. The place was empty. The spotlight still burned. I took my place. I said my poem. The empty room resounded. The walls heard my words. They were disgusted.

I ate a cinnamon roll. I was disgusted. I ran outside. In the street, another girl. The one with yellow hair tinged with green. Rat. She was known to me. She walked. I followed. She thought. I skulked in shadow.

She arrived at her house. I lurked. She went in. I went away. Back to the place of the poem. I said my poem again.

The cream for the coffee curdled. The cinnamon rolls turned moldy.

I said my poem again. The spotlight turned a sickly brownish-green.

I left the place. I returned to the streets and the moon.

I had a nice time.

"So what do you think about the werewolf?" I asked Winston Bongo as we walked home that night.

"It makes no sense to me," Winston said. "I suppose those beatniks are plenty superstitious."

"So you don't think there could be anything . . ."

Winston gave me an exasperated look. "I have an open mind," he said, "but I didn't see a werewolf or anything else. All I saw was that weird chick who waits on tables get all excited, and then the skinny poet hollered that it was a werewolf, and everybody scrammed. Just panic—that's all I saw."

"Yeah—well, that's what I think too," I said, "not that there couldn't be any such thing as a werewolf."

"I'm not saying I know for sure," Winston said, "I'm just saying that I, personally, have never seen one—and I didn't see one tonight either. What's more, I don't think anybody else did."

"I saw something," I said.

"You what?"

"I saw something—at least I think I may have. It was like a big shadow—just before Quicksilver hollered and cleared the place out. It was standing in the kitchen door. I just caught it out of the corner of my eye."

"You probably imagined it," Winston said.

"Probably. Only I don't think I imagined it."

"Sure you did. Besides, it's so dark in there any-way."

"Yeah—I guess."

We both walked a lot faster.

Rat headed for school. There was a strong wind coming off the lake. Particles of dust stung her face. Wastepaper and dead leaves swirled along the pavement. A bit of paper, a portion of a page from a paperback book, wrapped itself around her knee and was held there by the wind.

She plucked at the paper, grasped it for a moment, and let it go. Her eyes had fallen on the fragment—she had almost read the words—then it was gone. It tumbled in air, plastered itself against a tree, and then continued on its way.

It read:

This is the story of a werewolf in a great city in the present time. It is the story of the hopes and dreams of a boy whose future is limited to biting strangers and running through the streets. It is the story of a soul on fire, a youth of pure heart and low morals. It is the story of one who knows not what he does.

The page was the beginning of *The Sorrows of Young Werewolf* by K.E. Kelman, PH., a romantic account of the life of a werewolf. The book had been reviewed as a monstrosity, and was banned in most cities. Even that did not help its sales.

Of course, Rat knew nothing about any of this.

Breakfast with my parents—ah, bitter dull it was! The scrambled eggs and bacon were a-cold. My mother, while she ate, smoked cigarettes—and this was the boring story my father told:

"So you see, Walter, what with avocados costing as much as they did, even back in those days, I wondered just who you had to be to get them at wholesale prices, and where they were to be gotten. Well, it turned out that there's a big wholesale vegetable market way over on the west side—and anybody at all can buy there, as long as you buy in lots of a full case at a time. All this takes place early in the morning—more like the middle of the night. Well, I went over there on my bicycle, and I got a whole case of ripe avocados, and brought the thing home balanced on the handlebars. Of course I had more avocados than the family could eat before they (the avocados) started to rot, so it occurred to me to see if anyone in the neighborhood might want to buy some. They did. My prices were lower than the grocery store's, and my avocados had been picked out by an expert. Well, that's how I got started on my first avocado route when I was only fourteen."

This wasn't the first time I had heard the story of my father's avocado route. It has to be understood, my father is not a bad guy. What's more, he knows quite a lot of interesting stuff—the only trouble with him is that, if left to choose his own topics he will invariably choose to tell stories about avocados. My mother, for

28

her part, seems to like these stories. I guess that's why they got married in the first place.

Saturday morning breakfast can go on and on, and the safest thing to do is to get my father started on a topic other than avocados. You want him talking, you see, because it distracts from my mother's cooking. My father believes in my mother's cooking. He says it will prepare me for life. He says his mother cooked just like my mother, and that nothing in this world frightens him. To keep him from starting another avocado story, I thought it might be wise to ask him a question.

"Say, Dad, what do you know about werewolves?" I asked.

My father brightened up. I knew at once that I had hit pay dirt. He leaned back in his chair and looked up at the ceiling.

"What do I know about werewolves?" he said. "Let's see, I ought to know something about werewolves." I had struck the mother lode, I could tell. Obviously, he knew plenty about werewolves. I was going to get through breakfast without another word about avocados, and I'd have lots of information with which to astound Winston Bongo later.

"Now, by a werewolf, I assume you mean a lycanthrope, a person who turns into a wolf. This is all legendary, of course, although many people still believe in them. The Greeks told stories about wolf men. Their name for one was *lycanthropos*. The Romans called your werewolf *versipellis*, which means turn-skin—which was also an early English name for a werewolf—because his skin changes, you see. In French it's *loup-garou*, in German *wahrwolf*, and in Russian it's *volkodlak*. Werewolves seem to appear in almost every culture. The Navajos had 'em—and there's an African tradition of leopard men, which is the same sort of thing.

"There are a lot of different versions of how someone gets to be a werewolf. In some traditions the werewolf is a sorcerer or magician who deliberately changes himself into a wolf for whatever reason—just for fun, I suppose. However, in most versions of the story the person becomes a wolf by accident. A bite from another werewolf will do it, or coming upon werewolf flowers in the light of the full moon. There's a gypsy legend which goes like this:

> *Even a man who is pure in heart*
> *and says his prayers by night*
> *can become a wolf when the wolfbane blooms*
> *and the autumn moon is bright.*

"These days, most people know about werewolfery from the movies. My favorite is *The Werewolf of London*. You may have seen it at the Snark."

At this point, my father winked at my mother. I always deny that I snark out. It is part of the sport. My parents know that I snark out, but haven't actually gotten any proof. I insist that they insist irrationally that I snark, which of course I do, and they know I do—but there's no other way. My father always tries to trick me into admitting that I am a snarker. That was the intention of his remark about my having possibly seen *The Werewolf of London* at the Snark.

"I beg your pardon," I said, "I don't know what you mean."

"Well, never mind," my father said, "in *The Werewolf of London,* this outstanding English botanist goes to Tibet in search of a rare flower called *marifesa.* The marifesa blooms only by moonlight. The botanist is attacked by a werewolf who, for some reason, is looking for the same plant. The botanist gets bitten, thinks nothing of it, finds the flower, and brings it back to England. There, he intends to bring the flower to bloom by means of synthetic moonlight.

"He is visited by a Japanese scientist who, in actuality, is the very werewolf that attacked the botanist in Tibet. It turns out that the juice of the marifesa, squeezed onto the skin, is an antidote to the effects of werewolfism. Now, I got interested in the marifesa myself. I wondered if it was a real flower, or just something made up for the movie. I did a little research at the Blueberry Library, and what do you think I found out? Not only is there such a plant as the marifesa, but it's a distant relative of—guess what?"

I felt a sinking sensation.

"No fooling," my father said, "the marifesa is a member of the same family as the avocado. Isn't that interesting? Then I found out that there are just hundreds of Asian relatives of the avocado I never knew about."

It was hopeless. He was off again. Throughout this story, my mother had smoked cigarettes and listened with what appeared to be real interest. It was hard for me to believe that I was really the child of these people.

The phone rang. I ran to answer it. It was Winston Bongo calling to tell me to be outside in ten minutes. He had something he wanted to show me.

31

I told my parents I had to go out, and that I was sorry I couldn't stay and hear more about Asian relatives of the avocado.

"That's all right," my father said, "it is not your fault, my son."

I went downstairs to wait for Winston. There wasn't any sign of him in the street. Then I heard a noise like a soul in torment. It was a clicking and wheezing sound with a sort of low-pitched throbbing behind it. From around the corner came the thing that was making the noise. Winston was inside the thing. He pulled up in front of the apartment building. The thing made a high, piercing squeal, and then a loud thump.

"What is it?" I asked.

"It's a car!" Winston shouted over the clicking and wheezing of the motor.

"But just barely," I said. "Whose is it?"

"It's mine!" Winston said. "Get in—I'll take you for a ride."

I got in, first undoing the striped necktie that held the door shut. "Just knot that securely, and we'll be off," Winston said.

He put the car in gear, making a noise like a bunch of marbles being shaken in a can. The car shook all over, and then seemed to try to move forward. In a few seconds, it was clear that we were rolling. When we worked up to a brisk walking pace, Winston shot his arm out the window and merged into traffic. There was a lot of shouting and horn honking from the other drivers.

The car was unlike anything I'd ever seen. There was liberal rust inside and out, and sections of the body were covered with wide swatches of that gray metallic tape that sticks to anything. The seats were lumpy and covered with what appeared to be an old bedspread. A lot of wires hung down under the dashboard, and one of the dashboard knobs had been replaced by a pink eraser with a screw through it.

"You probably don't know what this is," Winston said. "It's a classic European luxury car—a Peugeot 403 Super Grand Luxe Extra—probably a 1958 or '59—my uncle doesn't remember."

"Is that where you got the car, from your uncle?"

"That's right. He gave it to me. All I had to come up with was money for insurance. What a great car this is!"

Winston's uncle was the Mighty Gorilla, a professional wrestler. He was a very cultured man, and had spent a lot of time in Europe, where, I assumed, he had gotten the luxury car.

"It's sort of past its prime, isn't it?" I asked.

"Oh, you mean because it looks a little beaten-up," Winston said, "that has nothing to do with the machinery. It has been neglected—for example, it stood half under water in a field for a couple of years—but these cars were built to take a beating. Listen to that engine!"

I listened to the engine. It sounded like a kitchen stove rolling down a hill.

In fact, we were trying to go up a hill—and not a very steep one. There was a line of cars behind us, honking.

"I didn't know you even had your license," I said.

"I just got it," Winston said. "My uncle was saving

this car to give to me as soon as I was legal. Just hand me that window crank—I'm feeling a little chilly." There was only one crank handle for the two front windows. I pulled it out of the door and handed it to Winston, who fitted it into the little hole and rolled up his window.

"What do you say we motor over to Rat's house?" he asked.

We hadn't seen Rat for a while. She hadn't shown up at the Snark lately, and had missed a rare screening of *The Terror of Tiny Town,* a western with an all-midget cast.

Rat's family is rich. They have a butler. They always call their butlers Heinz, and their butlers always wear Chinese robes. Nobody has ever explained why this is so. Heinz answered the door.

"Miss Rat is in her soundproof room," Heinz said. Rat's soundproof room is in the basement. She hangs out there, playing the most powerful monophonic hi-fi set in the state. There's a push-button, like a doorbell, that flashes a light inside the room—Rat wouldn't be able to hear anyone knocking.

When Rat opened the door, Winston said, "Come outside. There's something we want you to see."

Rat followed us into the street. "A Peugeot!" she said. "It's a '58 Super Grand Luxe Extra with independent transverse leaf-spring suspension, rack-and-pinion steering, sixty-four horsepower, and a maximum speed of eighty-one miles per hour. Not a bad set of wheels—whose is it?"

"It's mine," Winston said, "my uncle gave it to me."

"You ought to be able to get about twenty-six miles per gallon with this baby," Rat said, "if you've got it tuned properly. Open the hood and start it up."

Rat knows a lot about cars. Winston had forgotten that, and looked a little depressed thinking that Rat knew more about his new car than he did. He opened the hood and started the engine. Rat pulled a multi-blade Swiss knife out of her pocket and unfolded the small screwdriver. She listened to the engine, then reached in with the knife and did something. The engine sounded smoother at once.

"That was way out of adjustment," Rat said. "It should run a lot better now. You ought to leave it here for a few hours sometime—I'll go over it for you and get it running perfectly. Right now, why don't we go someplace? What do you say?"

Winston was obviously bugged. It must have pleased him that his car was running better, but the fact that Rat knew all about his car while Winston basically knew how to start the thing made him a little uncomfortable.

"We came over to take you for a ride," Winston said, "that was our intention in the first place. Is there anywhere in particular you'd like to go?"

"Let's drive out to Hamfat," Rat said.

Hamfat is a classy suburb where rich people live. I had driven through it maybe once or twice while going somewhere with my parents, but I didn't know anything about it.

"Hamfat is pretty far," Winston said.

"If the car breaks down, I can probably fix it," Rat said.

"Why do you want to go to Hamfat?" I asked Rat.

"I just want to go there," Rat said, "I've never been."

"I've never been either," Winston said. "We may as well go."

"May as well," I said.

We piled into the Peugeot and rumbled off toward the suburbs.

I sat in the back seat. Rat sat up front with Winston so she could listen to the engine. When she had listened to the engine enough, she wanted to play the radio. Winston told her it didn't work. She dove under the dashboard and fooled with some of the wires. In a minute or two, she had the radio playing. Rat found a New Wave/Country station and settled back in her seat, her arm out the window, beating time on the side of the car.

Grand Avenue takes you right out of Baconburg and into the suburbs. You pass through Porkington and Trottersville, and then you arrive in Hamfat. Starting in Trottersville, the road is lined on both sides with discount gas stations, fast-food restaurants, and stores with big parking lots. All the stores have huge signs you're supposed to see a mile away, except there are other signs sticking up in front of them—KIELBASA MART, FUDGE GIANT, SOCK CITY, UNDERWEAR WORLD, UNPAINTED SURGICAL APPLIANCE OUTLET, and CLAMS ARE US.

In the distance we saw a sign in the shape of a gigantic doughnut with skinny arms and legs which ended in feet wearing big Minnie Mouse shoes. The doughnut had a crown on top and a lady's face. "Hey!" Rat said. "There's Ms. Doughnut, where Quicksilver, the poet, works. Let's stop in and see if he's there."

"Aha!" Winston said. "So that's why you wanted to come out here!"

"No," Rat said. "I just happened to remember that Quicksilver works at the doughnut place."

"And you just happened to remember that the doughnut place is out here in Hamfat," Winston said. "We know you've got a crush on that skinny poet, and think the sun shines out of his earholes."

"Slow down," Rat said, "you'll go right past it."

"I haven't got enough money for a doughnut," Winston said.

"I'll buy you one," Rat said.

"I want a cup of coffee too," Winston said.

"O.K., you can have a cup of coffee."

"Walter wants a doughnut."

"Fine," Rat said, "Walter can have a doughnut too, you creep."

"Walter wants a cup of coffee," Winston said.

"Pull in there, you miserable mooch," Rat said. "I will buy you and Walter a doughnut and a cup of coffee each."

"I'm not a mooch," Winston said. "It isn't my idea to stop at Ms. Doughnut and visit your boyfriend—but if we're going in there, I don't want to stand around like a fool and not buy anything."

"Quicksilver is not my boyfriend," Rat said. "I am faithful to the memory of James Dean, as you know very well. You can quit with that sort of remark or the free doughnuts are off, see?"

"I'm not charging you anything to ride in my car," Winston said as he turned into the Ms. Doughnut parking lot.

Rat turned around in her seat. "Why are you his friend?" she asked me.

"He gets people to buy me doughnuts," I said.

"Cretins!" Rat said.

Jonathan Quicksilver was alone behind the counter. There were a couple of customers at the far end, dunking. It was pretty quiet. Two or three flies were buzzing around the racks of doughnuts. Quicksilver didn't remember us.

"Hi!" Rat said.

"Hi!" the poet said.

"She thinks you're wonderful," Winston said.

"You know my work?" Quicksilver asked.

"Oh, yes," Rat said. "I've read every poem in your book *I Am Cool.*"

"All *RIGHT!*" the poet said. "What will you three cultured beings have?"

Rat ordered a toasted-coconut doughnut and a light coffee. Winston ordered a mint doughnut and black coffee. I asked for a chocolate-covered, orange-marmalade filled doughnut and a coffee with double cream and double sugar.

Quicksilver filled our orders. "No charge for poetry lovers," he said in a whisper. "The boss isn't here."

"Hey, thanks, Mr. Quicksilver," Winston said. "We sure do love your poems."

"Seconds are on the house, if you can eat 'em," Quicksilver said.

"This guy is a prince," Winston said to me with his mouth full.

"What are you sensitive souls doing out here in the wasteland?" Quicksilver asked. By wasteland, I assumed he meant the suburb of Hamfat, which I was starting to like. For instance, there isn't a Ms. Doughnut in the city of Baconburg.

"We came to see you," Rat said.

40

Winston winked at me. "We came to pay homage to your genius," he said.

"Well, it's about time somebody did," Jonathan Quicksilver said. "Some of the other poets, who are jealous of me, you know, have been telling my fans that I work in the Ms. Doughnut all the way out in Swinesburg, twenty miles in the other direction. The poetry lovers go out there—can't find me—get upset—eat doughnuts—get sick—and finally are turned against me and my poems."

"That's a filthy shame!" Winston said.

"Those other poets are supposed to be my friends," Quicksilver said. "All they want to do is destroy me. You guys want to hear my newest poem?"

"Oh, yes!" Rat said. She was really enthusiastic. Jonathan Quicksilver poured some extra coffee into her cup.

"Okay, here goes," he said.

```
         THE WORLD OWES ME A LIVING 'CAUSE I'M SHORT
HEY

                  I DIDN'T ASK TO BE

                            SHORT

            NOBODY

            SAID TO ME

                                   HEY

                  DO YOU

                  WANT TO BE

                                A

                            SHRIMP

      IF THEY HAD

                  I WOULD HAVE SAID

                            NO

                        I WANT TO BE TALL

AND I DON'T WANT TO

                  WORK

                  EITHER

                       *
```

"God! That's beautiful!" Rat said.

"It is, isn't it?" Quicksilver said. "Any more doughnuts here?"

Winston had a mocha pistachio whole wheat, and I had a peppermint-stick guava with powdered sugar. Rat passed up a second doughnut, and was content just to gaze at Quicksilver with love and admiration.

After a while, Winston and I found her drooling on the skinny poet a little sickening—also we were feeling a bit queasy from the doughnuts. We wanted to get out of the doughnut shop, but Rat was going to have to be dragged away.

"Mr. Quicksilver," Winston asked, "can you suggest anything we ought to do while we're out here—in the wasteland?"

"Why don't you visit my guru?" Quicksilver asked. "He's always good for a few inspiring words of wisdom."

"You have a guru?" I asked.

"Yes, indeedy," Quicksilver said, "the Honorable Lama Lumpo Smythe-Finkel."

"The Honorable Lama Lumpo Smythe-Finkel?"

"My spiritual guide and teacher. You can usually find him at the mall on Saturdays—look for a guy with a long white beard and a saintly expression. He's the best."

"We'll look him up," Winston said.

"Give him my regards," Quicksilver said.

The Grand Mall was not what we expected. It was a couple of miles past the Ms. Doughnut where Quicksilver worked. We almost went right past it. All of us had been to the Mega-Mall in Swinesburg. That mall is huge. You can spend the whole day there and not see all the stores. There must be thirty places to buy jeans there. There are big trees growing indoors, a fountain as big as a swimming pool, Santa Claus at Christmas and the Easter Bunny at Easter. It's your regular, splendid, flashy, modern mall.

My father told me that untold thousands of dollars had been spent designing the Mega-Mall so that people shopping there would feel a certain way. He said they were intended to feel slightly fatigued and out-of-place and unimportant. He said that psychologists had been consulted about the lights, colors, the height of the ceilings, everything. The idea is that if you feel uncomfortable in just the right degree, you'll spend more money.

He said that just by making the lights flicker at a certain frequency, the designers of the mall could induce the average person to spend 11.3 percent more than if he was in his right mind.

My father didn't like the Mega-Mall because he felt there should have been a first-class greengrocer in a place as well planned as that.

The Grand Mall was completely unlike the Mega-Mall. The first thing we noticed was that there were hardly any people in it. There were a few shoppers walking around, but no huge crowds. Also, there were no vast bunches of kids hanging out the way there always are at the Mega-Mall. What was more, about half the spaces for stores had no stores in them.

There were iron gates across the fronts of the nonstores. Some of them still had signs up, left over from the last occupants: PROFESSOR POPCORN, THE JEANS GIANT, GORDON'S MODERN ORGANS, PHIL'S HOUSE OF FERRETS, FASHIONS OF GUAM, and BUGWORLD. It may have been that Bugworld sold bugs to people who collect bugs—or maybe it sold exterminator's supplies—roach traps and things like that. In any event, Bugworld was out of business.

The Grand Mall did not appear to have been designed by psychologists who wanted to make people spend more money. The people we saw there looked depressed, but they didn't appear to be spending anything. They drifted along, and the storekeepers were doing a lot of leaning and yawning.

We liked the place. The trees were small and obviously made of plastic, and the ceilings were low. There was a cheap linoleum in different colors and patterns on the floor, and the whole place was sort of grimy. It was a mall you could feel comfortable in.

The stores that were still in business were all sort of uninteresting. There were a couple of gift and card shops—the sort of place I never go into. There was a wood-burning stove store—nothing doing there. There was a health food store with an unhealthy-looking guy behind the counter. There was a dinky video arcade with about five machines—two of them out of order—and nobody playing. There was a frozen yogurt place. Winston and I took note of that in case the effects of the doughnuts should wear off. Rat will not eat yogurt. She says that if God had intended for us to eat spoiled milk He wouldn't have let us invent refrigerators.

All in all, at first glance, there was nothing of interest about the Grand Mall. What we liked about it was its very crumminess. We had been looking out for the Honorable Lama Lumpo Smythe-Finkel, Jonathan Quicksilver's guru. We'd had no luck finding him. Then we discovered the only interesting place in the Grand Mall, and the honorable lama, both at once.

What we discovered was a bookstore. The sign outside said HOWLING FROG—BOOKS OF THE WEIRD, and inside there was, in addition to a fat bald-headed guy behind the counter, a man with a flowing snowy-white beard.

"Welcome to Howling Frog—Books of the Weird," the fat bald guy said. "I am Howling Frog, the owner, general manager, clerk, stock boy, and janitor—and this is my good friend and spiritual guide, the Honorable Lama Lumpo Smythe-Finkel."

The guy's name was Howling Frog! Never in all my life had I heard such a neat name. I was afraid I was being impolite, but I had to ask, "Excuse me, your name . . . it's . . . I mean . . . are you by any chance an Indian?"

"So far as I know I am not," Howling Frog said, "neither East Indian, West Indian, nor Amerindian am I—although I have the greatest respect and admiration for all those peoples. Why do you ask?"

"It's just your name," I said, "it's such an unusual name."

"It's the name my father, the late Phineas Frog, gave me," Howling Frog said. "The Frogs, from whom I have the honor to be descended, are an illustrious family, mentioned often in American history—and Howling is a traditional name going back to my great-great-great grandfather, Howling Frog, who fought in the War of 1812, and later went out west to Illinois, where he was known as Yellow Dog Howling Frog. His son, Yowling Howling Frog, knew Dan'l Boone. There have been Howling Frogs around for a long time."

"Well, it's a name I never heard before," I said.

"Old American name," Howling Frog said.

"I'll take your word for it," I said.

"You can do so. A Frog never lies."

"What sort of bookstore is this?" Rat asked. She had been looking around while I talked with Howling Frog.

"What sort? What sort of bookstore is this? Lama, she wants to know what sort of bookstore this is. Why, you sweet little girl, this is the finest sort of bookstore there is—just the finest there is, that's all."

Winston and I both got alert when Howling Frog called Rat a sweet little girl. Nobody had ever addressed her like that to my knowledge, and it didn't seem to Winston or me that she was apt to like it. Rat had no problem about talking back to adults, and using some pretty outrageous language too. Apparently Howling Frog had made a big hit with her, because she didn't even snarl when he called her a sweet little girl. She just listened as he went on with his explanation.

"Books of the Weird is the bookstore in which you can find those books you never dreamed of finding, books you never knew existed. I have books about unheard-of places, seldom visited and practically unknown. I have books dealing with miraculous events and strange occurrences. I have books on obscure topics, such as knot-worship in fifteenth-century Switzerland, and how to tell a person's character by the shapes of his ears. And I specialize in scary books about ghosts, vampires, poltergeists, banshees, time travelers, voodooists, cultists, and Republican presidential candidates."

"Anything about werewolves?" I asked.

"I've got the best werewolf section in town," Howling Frog said.

"I'd like to have a look at it," I said.

"Too scary for kids," Howling Frog said. "What do you say, Lama?"

"Maybe not for these kids," the Honorable Lama Lumpo Smythe-Finkel said.

"Jonathan Quicksilver said to say hello to you," Winston said.

"My disciple?" the lama asked, all excited. "He's a great poet, did you know that?"

"We know," Rat said. "We've heard him read his poems."

"Ever hear this one?" the lama asked. "It's a beaut!"

THERE'S

SOMETHING

FLOATING

IN

MY

MILK

UGH

WHAT IS IT

OH

PLEASE

GOD

DON'T

LET

IT

BE

A

MOUSE

CAUSE

I

ALREADY

DRANK

SOME

*

"That's a great one, isn't it?"

"It sure is," Rat said. "That's in his book."

"I've got copies right here," Howling Frog said. "He's the sort of poet my customers like."

50

"You asked about werewolves," the lama said. "Why?"

"Why?"

"Why?"

"Why did I ask about werewolves?"

"Yes. Why did you ask about werewolves?"

"I'm just curious about them," I said. "My father and I were talking about werewolves this morning."

"Incredible!" Lama Lumpo Smythe-Finkel said.

"It is?"

"Yes. It is. It's incredible that you should mention werewolves just at this moment."

"Sure. I can see that. I can see that it would be . . . incredible . . . I mean . . . why is it incredible?"

"Why?"

"Why incredible that I should mention werewolves just at this moment."

"I'll tell you why," the lama said. "It's incredible because at this very moment I am having a strong psychic experience having to do with a werewolf."

"You are?"

"The strongest. I am getting werewolf signals plain as day. You know, as an official lama of the Serious Hat Order of Tibet and New Jersey, it is part of my job to be psychic as a bug. I read the future, read minds, get all sorts of telepathic promptings—the works. Right now I am getting powerful werewolf signals."

"Really?"

"You bet."

"Oh, this is very interesting," Howling Frog said. "I just love it when the lama goes all telepathic."

51

"What are the werewolf signals like?" I asked the lama.

"It's fairly horrible," the lama said. "Are you sure you want to know?"

"Yes, tell us," Rat said.

"Someone in this room is going to have dealings with a werewolf in the near future."

"Who? Which one in this room?" Howling Frog asked.

"I can't be sure," Lama Lumpo Smythe-Finkel said. "All I know is that it isn't me, for which I'm thankful—werewolves aren't nice."

"I guess not," Howling Frog said, "and you don't know which of us it is—the one who's going to meet the you-know-what."

"It might be all of you, for all I know," the lama said. "It's a nasty business."

"When is this likely to happen?" Howling Frog asked.

"It could be any minute—I don't know."

"I think I'll close up early today," Howling Frog said. "Here's a book for you kids—no charge."

Howling Frog handed us a book. Its title was *Coping with Werewolves*.

"Can you give me a ride back to my yurt?" the lama asked.

"Of course, Lama," Howling Frog said. "See you kids another time."

Howling Frog hustled us out of the store and closed the folding metal gate and locked it. He and the lama hurried down the mall and out of sight.

We looked at each other, a little worried. Speaking for myself, I can't say that I especially believed the

Honorable Lama Lumpo Smythe-Finkel. After all, he was just some bearded old bozo hanging out in a book-store for twinkies interested in strange topics. On the other hand, he seemed sort of sure of himself, as though he knew what he was talking about.

"Those guys are crazy, right?" I said.

"Right."

"Crazy."

Winston and Rat agreed with me. Those guys were crazy. "Besides," Winston said, breaking into my thoughts, "you mentioned werewolves first. If you hadn't said anything about them, and *then* the lama had brought the subject up, that would be different."

"You think he's a fake then?"

"Sure," Winston said, "all those lamas are fakes."

"Ugh," Rat said. "Look, it's Scott Feldman."

You could see right away that Scott Feldman was a creep. He was incredibly, unbelievably neat and tidy. His hair was neatly combed, he had eyeglasses of which the lenses were singularly clean, and the frames appeared to have been polished. His sweater looked brand-new and it was tucked into the waistband of his trousers, which were spotless and had sharp creases down the front of each leg. He was leaning against a wall, with his hands in his pockets in such a way that he didn't wrinkle his pants, and he had the sole of one new-looking shoe against the wall. He was easy to hate. Scott Feldman had the most amazing and unusual expression, I'd ever seen—a sort of hypnotic stare. It made you numb and turned your stomach.

Evidently, Rat knew Scott Feldman from school. He called her Miss Matthews.

"Hello, Miss Matthews," Scott Feldman said. "I am delighted and surprised to see you here in the mall. I am Scott Feldman, your classmate, in case you don't remember me."

"I remember you," Rat said.

"Thank you," Scott Feldman said. Then, extending his hand, he said to me, "I am Scott Feldman, I am pleased to make your acquaintance."

I shook hands with Scott Feldman. "Walter Galt," I said.

Then Scott Feldman did the same thing—introduced himself to Winston and shook hands with him. Then he offered a compliment to Rat: "You are looking very pretty today, Miss Matthews."

"You want me to punch your face?" Rat said, in her prettiest voice.

"Hey! No violence, please!" Scott Feldman said. "I don't like to fight or get my clothes dirty. Otherwise," he said, sort of winking at Winston and me, "I am a regular guy."

To Rat he said, "Perhaps you will remember that I called you on the telephone once."

"You called me on the telephone about fifteen times," Rat said, "and I told you fifteen times that I don't want to go with you to the zoo to see the snakes at feeding time."

"You missed a treat," Scott Feldman said.

"You're a bizzarro," Rat said.

"No, I'm not," Scott Feldman said, "I'm a regular highly intelligent high school student with many interests and a healthy admiration for you, Miss Matthews."

"I'm getting a frozen yogurt," I said. "Anybody else want a yogurt?"

"I don't eat yogurt," Scott Feldman said. "Yogurt, like milk, cheese, and all other dairy products, is a mucus-producing food. It isn't good to have too much mucus."

"Maybe I'll skip the yogurt," I said, and to Rat, "your friend is fairly disgusting."

"Don't call him that!" Rat said. "Don't call him my friend. I can't help who I go to school with."

"I think she likes me quite a lot," Scott Feldman said. "I'm the cutest and best-dressed boy in school."

"Let's kill him," Winston said. It was the first thing he'd said since meeting Scott Feldman.

"I assume you're only kidding," Scott Feldman said, "but just in case, I think it only fair to tell you that I have studied Subi-waza with the Subi-waza master of New Jersey. It's the deadliest martial art. I took a course by mail, and I am now a lethal weapon."

"Only kidding, of course," Winston said, and then he whispered to me, "I mean it, let's kill him."

"Did you know that Bugworld has moved?" Scott Feldman asked.

I wasn't surprised to learn that Scott Feldman had an interest in bugs. He was what I would have pictured as the typical customer at Bugworld.

"How did you get all the way out here, Scott?" Rat asked.

"I took the shoppers' bus this morning," Scott Feldman said. "Now that I'm here, and Bugworld's not open, I have to wait three more hours for a bus to take me back—you didn't come in a car, did you?"

Rat said no, and I said yes, both at the same time. Scott Feldman chose to hear my reply. "Good! I can ride back with you kids."

"That will be ducky," Winston said.

ANOTHER MYSTERIOUS OUTBREAK OF VIOLENCE STRUCK THE BACONBURG AREA LAST NIGHT. . . . MILTON PAPESCU OF HAMFAT SURPRISED SOMEONE—OR SOMETHING—IN THE ACT OF WRECKING HIS 1978 CHEVROLET MALIBU. . . . WHEN MR. PAPESCU CAME OUT OF THE SHPILKIE TOWER, BACONBURG'S TALLEST BUILDING, WHERE HE HAD BEEN WORKING LATE IN HIS OFFICE, HE FOUND THAT SOMETHING WAS RIPPING THE DOOR OFF HIS CAR. . . . PAPESCU SHOUTED, AND A LARGE, DARK, INDISTINCT SHAPE LOPED OFF AT HIGH SPEED. PAPESCU WAS DISTRAUGHT. . . .

(*Shot of Papescu—owner of wrecked car*)

Papescu: I COULDN'T SAY IT WAS HUMAN. . . IF IT WAS A HUMAN IT WAS A VERY BIG ONE. . . . I HOLLERED, "HEY! STOP THAT!" AND THIS THING. . . . I DON'T KNOW WHAT IT WAS. . . . I WAS LOOKING RIGHT AT IT, BUT SOMEHOW I CAN'T REMEMBER WHAT I SAW. . . . I EVEN REMEMBER KNOWING THAT I WOULDN'T BE ABLE TO SAY WHAT I SAW. . . . THIS SOUNDS CRAZY, BUT I THINK I WAS HYPNOTIZED BY THAT THING. . . . ANYWAY, WHEN I HOLLERED, IT LOOKED UP. . . . THEN IT SORT OF LOPED OFF.

Voice of interviewer: LOPED?

Papescu: YOU KNOW, LOPED. . . . IT LOPED OFF, AND I WAS LEFT WITH MY CAR IN THE SHAPE YOU SEE IT IN.

(*Shot of car with Papescu's voice over*)

IT'S A MESS. . . . THE DOOR IS RIPPED OFF. . . . THE STEERING WHEEL IS BENT DOUBLE. . . . THE UPHOLSTERY IS ALL TORN UP, AND THE INSIDE HAS THIS FUNNY SMELL . . . LIKE . . .

57

Voice of interviewer: LIKE WHAT?

Papescu: IT SMELLS LIKE DOG SPIT. . . . YOU KNOW, DROOL. . . . I HAVE THIS GIANT SCHNAUZER, AND HIS DROOL SMELLS A LITTLE LIKE THAT, ONLY NOT SO STRONG.

Voice of interviewer: ANOTHER ACT OF UNEXPLAINED VANDALISM IN OUR AREA. . . . BACK TO YOU, BOB.

(*Shot of Bob Pontoon, newscaster, in studio*)

Bob: THIS IS THE FIFTEENTH INCIDENT OF VANDALISM IN THE GREATER BACONBURG AREA THIS YEAR. . . . NINE CARS HAVE BEEN WRECKED. . . . POWER POLES HAVE BEEN KNOCKED DOWN. . . . AND THE STATUE OF FREE ENTER-PRISE IN FRONT OF BACONBURG CITY HALL IS MISSING. . . . IN FIVE INSTANCES SOMEONE OR SOMETHING WAS SEEN. . . . AN AMORPHOUS DARK SHAPE, WHICH COULD NOT BE PROPERLY DESCRIBED OR REMEMBERED. . . . IN EVERY CASE, THE EVENTS HAVE TAKEN PLACE DURING A FULL MOON.

BACONBURG AND AREA POLICE ARE STUMPED.

(*Shot of Police Chief Cloney*)

Cloney: THIS THING HAS GOT US STUMPED.

Bob: LOCAL AUTHORITIES HAVE BEEN SWAMPED BY SUGGESTIONS FROM MEMBERS OF THE PUBLIC AS TO WHAT IS CAUSING THESE BIZARRE EVENTS. . . . EVERYTHING FROM SUNSPOTS TO AN EXTRATERRESTRIAL TO THE WRATH OF GOD TO A WEREWOLF HAS BEEN SUGGESTED. . . .

WHAT IS BEHIND THESE MYSTERIOUS DESTRUCTIVE ACTS? TUNE IN TO OUR SPECIAL BROADCAST FOLLOWING THE ELEVEN O'CLOCK NEWS.

(*Shot of Papescu's ruined car with announcer's voice over*)

WATCH "THE BACONBURG HORROR" TONIGHT AT 11:30.

(*Shot of Bob Pontoon*)

58

Bob: AND THAT'S ALL THE NEWS OF BACONBURG. . . . STAY TUNED TO CHANNEL 52 FOR NEWS AS IT HAPPENS. SEE YOU AT 11:00 AND 11:30 WITH THE FULL STORY OF "THE BACONBURG HORROR."

(*Cut to deodorant commercial*)

The ride home was fairly ghastly. Scott Feldman talked about good grooming and personal hygiene. Winston and Rat moaned and ground their teeth. I looked through the book Howling Frog had given us, *Coping with Werewolves*. It was by someone named K.E. Kelman, PH. PH. stands for phantomologist, it turns out. This guy, K.E. Kelman, PH., claimed to have had vast experience with werewolves in all parts of the world. He said that werewolves were generally misunderstood creatures—so what if they bite someone once in a while? Dogs do that, and they are considered man's best friend.

K.E. Kelman, PH., went on to tell anecdotes about werewolves he had known. He told about the singing werewolf of Budapest, and the time he ate supper with a werewolf in Kazakhstan.

Kelman also claimed that many famous people were, in reality, werewolves. He said that Beethoven was one, also Dostoevsky, and Queen Victoria, Thomas Jefferson, Sigmund Freud, Mozart, Martin Luther, and Walter Cronkite.

I didn't get to read the whole book—I just skipped around. Also, I kept getting distracted by Scott Feldman's running commentary on the use of shoe trees and the responsibility of teenagers to help their families by taking care of their clothes.

After a while, Rat and Winston became openly insulting, and told Scott to shove his shoe trees and so forth. It didn't have the slightest effect. The only way to deal with Scott Feldman would have been to render him unconscious. Rat was talking about doing that when we arrived at Scott's house and dropped him off.

"I certainly had a good time," Scott Feldman said. "I hope we can do this again very soon."

"Just as soon as it snows in hell, Scott," Winston said.

"Or even sooner," Scott said.

"Get knotted," Rat said.

"And it was a special pleasure getting to see you again, Miss Matthews," Scott Feldman said.

"Step on the gas," Rat said to Winston.

Our next stop was Rat's house. "Let me take that book," she said to me. Rat hadn't shown any interest in the book or the werewolf topic until now. I handed her the book.

"I want to read it next," I said.

She got out of the car. "It was almost fun," she said.

The scene is the great council chamber of the Baconburg City Hall. The curtains are drawn, and a group of men is gathered around a table, lit by a single lamp. Their faces are grim. The mayor and the city council, the chief of police, representatives from the military, the FBI, and the state and federal governments are present. Dr. Bogenswerfer, Professor of Classical Lycanthropy at the University of Baconburg, is speaking.

"Gentlemen, I have given this matter prolonged and careful thought. I have consulted my books, and I have sought the opinions of my learned colleagues. I am sure. I can safely stake my professional reputation on my conclusions in this matter. What we have here, confronting us in the greater Baconburg area, are manifestations of the activity of a werewolf!

"Ordinary measures will be of no avail, for the werewolf stalks by night, and is all but invisible to the human eye. He is fleet of foot and vile-tempered. No person—and more to the point—no property is safe when one of these moon-crazed creatures is about. It is a werewolf, gentlemen, and you may quote me."

Professor Bogenswerfer sits down. Mayor Beesley speaks.

"If you are so sure it's a werewolf—and nobody else has come up with a better explanation—can you tell us how to deal with it?"

Dr. Bogenswerfer speaks.

"As to knowing how to deal with it—that is out of

my line. As a classical lycanthropist, it is within the purview of my specialty to know what has been written and said about werewolves in the past. I am also acquainted with all the means of discerning a werewolf—although this is the first time I've ever had to consider a real one—and I know a lot of werewolf poetry by heart. However, as to what to do with one—I haven't a clue.

"However, there is one man—a shabby sort of scholar, if you know what I mean—who has had some experience with the actual thing. I mean, this fellow is a terrible writer, full of vague sentiment and odd-sounding ideas, but he has, I believe, seen a werewolf, and knows what to do with one. Perhaps you would be interested in contacting him. He can't tell you much about the history of lycanthropy—but he might possibly tell you how to get the werewolf to stop pulling the doors off automobiles."

"Who is this man, and where can we find him?"

"His name is K.E. Kelman, PH. His credentials, while not the very best, are nonetheless authentic. As to where he can be found—there I cannot help you. I don't even know if Professor Kelman is still alive. The last I heard of him was that he had delivered a paper on the best way to remove werewolf-spit at the University of Kuala Lumpur."

The man from the FBI speaks. "If this K.E. Kelman, PH., still lives on Earth, we can find him."

"Good," says Mayor Beesley. "Do so. It may be the best chance we have."

She walks in beauty like a bat
A lizard, monster, or a ghoul;
This one with hair of green, this Rat;
She is the neatest girl in school.

She has an underground lair. Good idea. It is very silent. Another good idea. The windows are covered with cork. An extremely good idea. No sound from the outside can get in. What a good idea! No sound from the inside can get out. A really wonderful idea!

It's difficult to get into the lair. The door is locked. It would be too obvious to pull it off its hinges. Once I am inside I might reveal myself to her—wouldn't that be fun? And if she screams, no one will hear. And if she tells the story, who would believe it? Perhaps I will tell her my poem.

I've never told my poem to a living human—who lived.

It turned out that my mother knew Jonathan Quicksilver slightly. She was going to high school at night, and so was he. My mother had never finished high school. She quit in her senior year to go to Peru and help harvest the avocados. That was where she met my father.

Jonathan Quicksilver was doing high school at night, in order to get to be a citizen. It turns out he was from someplace in Europe. My mother didn't know where—just some little country in the Carpathian Mountains was all she remembered. I was surprised, because Quicksilver didn't speak with an accent. Anyway, he was in her civics class.

All of this came up when I was telling my parents about my day in Hamfat, and the things I had seen in the suburbs.

My father, predictably, latched onto the weirdest part of the story. He was very interested in knowing what I thought of the Honorable Lama Lumpo Smythe-Finkel. He asked a lot of questions. I suggested that he come out to the Grand Mall with me sometime and meet the lama—I had the impression he was there every Saturday. My father reminded me that he couldn't make it—he was taking a course in auto mechanics, which met on Saturdays. He belonged to a Honda Civic car owners' club, and every Saturday morning, after breakfast, he left the house with his Honda Civic textbook and his bag of tools.

"So what was your impression of the honorable lama, son?" my father asked. "These holy men from the East can be very amazing, I believe."

"I think the lama comes from New Jersey," I said, "and my impression of him was that he probably didn't know what he was talking about."

My father looked disappointed. "Sometimes these fellows are very deep," he said, "appearances can be deceiving."

"My friends Winston and Rat thought he was a schnook too," I said.

"Really, you ought to keep an open mind," my father said, "some of these fellows have really amazing mystical powers."

"I don't think this one had any more mystical powers than you have," I said.

"Aum? Is that so?" my father asked.

... and so, after so many years, and so many adventures with our friends the werewolves, the author has come to think of the lycanthrope as just another misunderstood soul. Werewolves abound in every society, and are slowly starting to gain acceptance as being loyal, clean, thrifty, reverent, trustworthy, and honest—good family people—and possessed of a sense of humor.

The author hopes that the reader of this little book will try to show some understanding the next time he meets a werewolf—and even in the unlikely event that there should be a bit of tooth-play, to remember that this is just the werewolf's way of saying "I like you." So, dear reader, the next time something big and furry and horrible gets you by the leg, just remember the old lycanthropian greeting, *"Grrrrrrrrrowf!"* You may be at the beginning of a beautiful friendship.

Rat was reading from Professor Kelman's book, *Coping with Werewolves.* As she read the book she became aware of a strange sensation—it was as though someone was in the room with her. At first she dismissed it as mere imagination, but the feeling persisted, and grew stronger.

After a while, Rat felt as though she wanted to scream—she didn't know why.

Just as Rat lost her nerve, and flew through the

door of her soundproof chamber, she had the briefest look at . . . something . . . nothing . . . a thick place in the air . . . a shadow where there shouldn't have been a shadow.

"That's good enough for me," Rat said. She picked up the phone in the hall and dialed Walter Galt's number.

"Walter," she said into the receiver, "get Winston and meet me at the Dharma Buns in an hour. We've got werewolf trouble."

Rat was waiting for us when we arrived at the Dharma Buns Coffee House. "Have a seat," she said, "I've ordered coffee."

"What's up?" I asked.

"Plenty," Rat said. "I think there's a werewolf around."

"That's what a lot of people have been saying," Winston said, "what makes you think it's so?"

"It was in my room," Rat said.

Winston and I looked at each other. "It was in your room? And you saw it?"

"I didn't exactly see it," Rat said. "I sort of sensed it—and I did see something. That is, I failed to see something. It was a weird sensation. It was like this— imagine that you know I'm sitting here, and all of a sudden you can't see me, but you sort of can see the space I'm sitting in. It's hard to explain."

"That's how it was when I sort of saw something the first night we ever came here," I said.

"You saw something that night?"

"Sort of . . . it was when Quicksilver hollered were-wolf and everybody cleared out. I sort of saw something standing in the kitchen door. Winston said it was nothing."

"Winston is a bugwit," Rat said, looking at Winston. "You probably did see something—sort of."

"You know, the fact that everybody sitting around this place ran without a second's hesitation is interesting," I said. "It's as if they all believed in werewolves, and had maybe had some experience with them—I mean, we didn't get up and run, but they all did."

"Here comes the waitress, the one who screamed," Winston said. "Let's ask her what she knows."

The depressed-looking waitress with the white makeup was bringing our coffee.

"Say," Winston said. "Remember the night when you saw something in the kitchen, and let out a scream?"

"Oh, yes, the werewolf," the waitress said, "it took me by surprise."

"How did you know it was a werewolf?" Winston asked.

"What else could it have been?" the waitress said.

"Have you ever seen a werewolf before?" Rat asked.

"Have you ever seen a live mastodon?" the waitress asked.

"No."

"But if one walked in here right now, you wouldn't have any doubts about what it was, would you?"

"No, I guess not."

"Well, there you are," the waitress said. She collected for the coffee and left.

"She's no help," Winston said.

"Of course not," Rat said, "werewolves are fast and tricky—I just got finished reading that book about them. What we need is a real werewolf expert."

"How about the Honorable Lama Lumpo Smythe-Finkel?" I suggested. "He seems to know something about them."

"We need somebody with a scientific approach," Rat said. "I think we ought to get in touch with the guy who wrote the book, K.E. Kelman, PH."

"The phantomologist?"

"Why not? If we've got a real werewolf running around loose, he should be interested, and we need some help. I, personally, do not want the thing turning up in my room anymore. Maybe K.E. Kelman, PH., can get rid of the thing for us."

"That makes sense to me," I said. "How do we go about finding the guy?"

"That shouldn't be much of a problem," Rat said.

Federal Bureau of Investigation
Missing Scientist Division
Dillinger Office Building
Washington, D.C.

The Honorable Lance Beesley
Mayor, City of Baconburg
City Hall
Baconburg

Dear Mayor Beesley:

Pursuant to your request, this office has undertaken exhaustive measures to maximize the location potential of one K.E. Kelman, PH.

We have optimized collateral assistance with our corresponding agencies in other countries, and have substantiated the financial refurbishment of various non-agency informational sources as well.

We are happy to report to you that our undertaking has been a consistent penetration of all informational matrices to be considered in relation to the parameters of our assignment.

All agency, non-agency, and peripheral personnel participating in the project have demonstrated maximum inter-cooperation and professionalism.

We feel certain that our output has been exhaustive and mega-effective.

K.E. Kelman, PH., either does not exist, does not exist in any form correlative to documentation provided this agency, or has ceased to exist, or never existed. In short, we can't find him.

Your FBI stands ready to serve you in any meaningful way within the purview of our constitutional responsibility.

Yours truly,

A. Platt Fleischkopf
Agent

72

"Good news," Rat said: "K.E. Kelman, PH., lives right here in Baconburg."

"How do you know that?" I asked her.

"I looked him up in the phone book," she said. "He lives on Talbot Court, which is not far from Bignose's Cafeteria. I thought we might call him up, and ask him to meet us there."

"Good idea," Winston said, "that way, if he's too weird, we can just run."

"That's not the idea at all," Rat said. "I just thought it would be sort of polite, and businesslike, if we bought him a cup of coffee and a pastry."

"Now, this was your idea," Winston said.

"Right, right . . . save your breath," Rat said. "I'm paying for the coffee and pastry, you impossibly cheap slob, so spare me the usual whining and carrying on."

Winston does always whine and carry on when money is about to be spent. I, for my part, am willing to pay for my own refreshments, but Winston will never allow that. I suppose if I paid for myself it would call even more attention to the fact that Winston exploits Rat just because she's rich. In return for always buying him coffee and food, Rat gets to constantly remind Winston that he's a pathological cheapskate. They have a kind of symbiosis, I suppose. I get the best deal of all—free eats, and nothing on my conscience.

"So call him up," Rat said. "Here's a dime."

"Why me?" Winston asked.

"So you won't be useless," Rat said. "Now call."

Winston dialed. We had been standing in the street outside the Snark Theater, near a pay phone. "Uh, is this K.E. Kelman, PH.?" Winston said into the phone. Apparently it was. "This is about a werewolf," Winston said. "No, it isn't a joke. We want to talk to you about a werewolf. My friends and I. Yes. Do you know Bignose's Cafeteria on Lower North Aufzoo Street? Sure, we can be there in ten minutes—maybe fifteen. O.K." Winston replaced the receiver. "He wants to meet us right away," he said.

It was just a short drive to Lower North Aufzoo Street, where Bignose's Cafeteria was. I was happy to be going there. It was a place I'd first visited the time Rat's uncle, a mad scientist named Flipping Hades Terwilliger, had disappeared, and we were looking for him. Bignose's is the only place I know in Baconburg where you can get Napoleons—that's a really fantastic pastry, at least the ones Bignose serves are fantastic.

The Peugeot had been parked across the street from the Snark, where we'd caught the early evening show—Murnau's *Sunrise* and *Gidget Gets Sick,* a couple of classics.

We found another good parking place outside of Bignose's. Winston was very particular about where he parked—it had to be under a streetlight. "There are a lot of thieves who specialize in classic cars," he said.

When we entered Bignose's the place was empty. Bignose was there, of course—he's unmistakable with the nose—and there was the lady who runs the cash register. There was no sign of K.E. Kelman, PH., or anybody else. There wasn't even anybody in the street outside.

"Hello, kids," Bignose said, "I haven't seen you for a while—you want the usual?"

Winston looked at Rat. Rat said nothing. "You having something?" he asked her.

"I don't think so," Rat said, "I had a big supper."

Winston thought for a while. I happened to know

that he loved Bignose's Napoleons better than anything. "Well, I'm going to have a Napoleon and a cup of coffee," Winston said to Bignose.

"Who's paying?" Rat asked.

Winston hesitated. It was clear from Rat's expression that she wasn't offering to pay for Winston's snack.

"Me. I'm paying," Winston said.

"In that case, make it three, Bignose—three Napoleons and three coffees. Thanks, Winston."

"That will be three-seventy-five," Bignose said.

Winston looked confused. He was trapped. Rat had trapped him. "That's what women are," he said to me, "exploiters and leeches." He paid Bignose and we carried our Napoleons and coffees to a table.

Winston was bugged. I was happy. I had yet to pay for my own food when I went anywhere with these two. "Shouldn't we have gotten a coffee and a Napoleon for K.E. Kelman, PH.?" I asked.

"Wait to see if he shows up," Winston said. "He's already late."

"I've been waiting for ten minutes," a voice from somewhere said, "and I would like a coffee, extra light, and a Napoleon, if the young man would be so kind."

We looked around. The place was still empty. "Who said that?" Winston asked.

"You are the parties who wish to meet with K.E. Kelman, are you not?" the voice said. This time we were able to locate it. It was coming from under the table.

"Are you under the table?" Rat asked.

"Yes, I am under the table. And now I am coming out," the voice said. A tall man in a raincoat appeared

76

from under the table, pulled up a chair, and sat down.

"And you are K.E. Kelman, PH.?" Rat asked.

"I am he," the man in the raincoat said. "Now don't let me stop you from enjoying your pastry—just dig in, and I'll start in on mine as soon as the young man brings it to me."

Winston went to the counter to get K.E. Kelman, PH., his Napoleon and coffee.

"Why were you under the table?" I asked.

"I have my reasons," K.E. Kelman, PH., said, "but let's not talk about me. Why did you want to meet with me?"

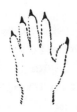

"You said something about a werewolf when you called," K.E. Kelman, PH., said. He was delicately working through his Napoleon. His beard was full, but neatly trimmed. He was bald on top and had shoulder-length hair. He kept his raincoat on, and buttoned, and he had a monstrous furled umbrella hooked over the back of his chair. There wasn't a sign of rain—and it hadn't rained for days.

"Yes," Rat said, "I'm pretty sure I sort of saw it."

"Not surprising," K.E. Kelman, PH., said. "There's one around these days. Quite a few people have had encounters with him."

"How do you know it's a him?" Rat asked.

"Quite so," K.E. Kelman, PH., said, "him or her . . . although female werewolves are rare indeed. I'd be pleased and delighted if this one should turn out to be a lady."

"Woman," Rat said.

"Oh, quit it already," Winston said.

"Take back what you said about women being exploiters and leeches," Rat said.

"Anything to stop the feminist rhetoric," Winston said. "It kills conversation. I take back what I said."

"As I was saying," K.E. Kelman continued, "there's a werewolf about. All the reports point to the same thing. The astrological conditions are right. It's the right time of year. There hasn't been a werewolf in this vicinity for more than thirty years—which means one is overdue. And my mother says she's been getting pains in her left big toe."

"Your mother?"

"My mother, Mrs. Lydia L. Kelman, is the finest little werewolf predictor in the state. By the way, you haven't introduced yourselves."

"I am Bentley Saunders Harrison Matthews," Rat said, "but you may call me Rat. This is Walter Galt, and this is our host, Winston Bongo."

"I didn't know I was going to have to pay for everything," Winston said.

"I'm pleased to meet all of you," K.E. Kelman, PH., said. "Now about this werewolf—what exactly is it you want me to do? Do you want to be introduced to the werewolf, or what?"

"Well . . . we want to get rid of it," Rat said.

"Get rid of it? Why?"

"I mean, it's a werewolf, isn't it?" Rat said.

"So I believe," K.E. Kelman, PH., said, "but has it done you any harm?"

"It was in my room!" Rat said.

"Probably it likes you," said the phantomologist. "Couldn't you think of it as a big friendly dog which is also a human being at times, and potentially very dangerous?"

"No!" Rat said. "I do not want anything of the kind turning up in my room. It's creepy."

"Well, I suppose I'll have to get my mother to werewolf-proof your room."

"Your mother?"

"Oh, yes. Mother is a whiz at that sort of thing. She'll come around and werewolf-proof your room for you. It doesn't cost a thing. Mother is rather old, you

79

see, and she just does things like that to keep busy. If you'll give me your address and telephone number, I'll have Mother get in touch with you. She'll do the were-wolf-proofing, and that will be the end of your troubles—and we won't have had to bother the poor werewolf."

"How do I know this will work?" Rat asked.

"My mother, before she retired, was known professionally as Lydia LaZonga—I trust that name means something to you." K.E. Kelman raised his eyebrows.

"As a matter of fact it doesn't," Rat said.

"Lydia LaZonga was known, in her day, as the world's foremost ghost finder, spook chaser, hoodoo remover, and general, all around, freestyle psychic. That is my mommy."

"Gee," Winston said.

"You may well say gee, young man. Mommy is the best."

"I suppose we should give it a try," Rat said.

"You won't be sorry," said K.E. Kelman, PH.

THE BACONBURG HORROR STRIKES AGAIN! LATE LAST NIGHT, SOMEONE OR SOMETHING BROKE INTO THE PORKINGTON FREE LIBRARY AND MADE A HORRIBLE MESS OF THE POETRY SECTION. BOOKS WERE STREWN EVERYWHERE, AND BOOKSHELVES WERE OVERTURNED. THE CARD CATALOGS WERE TURNED UPSIDE DOWN, AND MANY OF THE CARDS APPEAR TO HAVE TOOTH MARKS ON THEM.

HAVOC WAS PLAYED WITH THE RUBBER STAMPS, AND THERE WAS ONE UNUSUAL CLUE—IN THE FOYER OF THE LIBRARY, WRITTEN WITH WHAT APPEARS TO HAVE BEEN A CLAW PRESSED REPEATEDLY AGAINST A RUBBER STAMP INK PAD, WAS THIS PHRASE:

"I wander'd lonely as a shroud . . ."

PORKINGTON POLICE FORENSIC EXPERTS ARE STUDYING THE CLUE.

RUMORS THAT THE BACONBURG HORROR IS A WEREWOLF OR SOME SIMILAR SUPERNATURAL THING CONTINUE TO CIRCULATE. MAYOR LANCE BEESLEY, WHEN ASKED FOR COMMENT, SAID . . .

(*Shot of Mayor Beesley*) "NOTHING OF THE KIND. WE HAVE HAD EXTENSIVE CONSULTATION WITH THE FBI, CRIMINAL EXPERTS OF EVERY KIND, AND PROFESSOR BOGENSWERFER OF THE UNIVERSITY. WE ARE CERTAIN THAT NO SUCH THING AS A WEREWOLF EXISTS. THESE ACTS OF LAWLESSNESS ARE THOSE OF AN ORDINARY PERSON WITH A SICK MIND, AND WE WILL APPREHEND HIM VERY SOON. THERE IS NOTHING TO WORRY ABOUT. YOUR PUBLIC SERVANTS ARE ON THE JOB."

(*Bob Pontoon in the studio*) THAT'S THE LATEST ON THE BACONBURG HORROR. KEEP TUNED FOR LATE-BREAKING BULLETINS AS THEY HAPPEN.

(*Cut to commercial for home burglar alarms*)

(*Cut to commercial for stainless steel window shutters*)

(*Cut to commercial for mad dog repellent*)

(*Cut to commercial for discount flights to Australia*)

(*Bob Pontoon in studio*) AND THAT'S ALL THE NEWS OF BACONBURG. . . . SEE YOU TOMORROW.

The Dharma Buns Coffee House is nearly empty, as are all places where people have been accustomed to gather at night. The panic surrounding the mysterious events connected with the so-called Baconburg Horror is at its peak. People have taken to locking themselves in after dark.

So it is that Jonathan Quicksilver has a scanty audience for his newest poem:

```
    I COME FROM OLD TRANSYLVANEE
                    WHEN I WAS JUST A
                        LITTLE
                        BOY

AND
    MY
        OLD
            TRANSYLVANEE
                    MOMMEE
                        SAID
                        TO
                        ME
                        SON
                        SHE
                        SAID
            LOOK OUT FOR
                    THEM
                    WEREWOLF
                    HE
                        TAKE
                            A BIG BITE
                        OUT YOU TOOSHEE
```

```
HE
   PULL
       YOU
            LEG
               OFF
                  YOU
                     AND BEAT
                          YOU
                          ON
                          YOU
                          HEAD WITH
                               IT.
WEREWOLF IS NO JOKE
                     MY
                     LITTLE
                     SONNEE
SO MAYBE
        BETTER WE
                  EMIGRATE OUTTA
                            THIS
                            PLACE

                           *
```

Even though this will later be regarded as Quick-silver's finest poem, it finds no favor with the audi-ence. This is often the case with great Art.

"Big deal. Big phantomologist. Five whole dollars I spent in that place, and what's the result? His mommy is going to werewolf-proof your silly room." Winston was utterly disgusted.

"Well, I was sort of hoping for something a little more conclusive myself," Rat said.

"I had a good time," I said.

"Shut up," Rat and Winston said.

"Look," I said, "maybe Lydia LaZonga, or whatever her name is, can really do something for you."

"Maybe, but I doubt it," Rat said.

"It's your best bet," I said.

"It's all I've got," Rat said, "and it seems like nothing. Now I've got to go home and wonder if that weird thing is going to turn up again."

"K.E. Kelman, PH., didn't seem to be too worried," I said.

"K.E. Kelman, PH., is a dingdong!" Rat said. "He likes werewolves! He thinks they're cute! He wishes a werewolf would turn up in *his* room!"

"Now, am I correct in assuming that the werewolf didn't turn up in your bedroom, but in the soundproof room in the basement where you hang out all the time, is that right?" Winston asked.

"So?"

"So don't go down there. If the werewolf turns up upstairs, you can give out with a holler and wake up the house. From all accounts it seems to run away whenever anybody sees it."

"So you think the werewolf is shy, do you?" Rat asked.

"It keeps moving," Winston said.

"That's not very much comfort," Rat said.

"That's the best I can do," Winston said. "Unless you would like Walter and me to come and spend the night with you."

"Excellent idea," Rat said.

Winston leered.

"Spare me the juvenile sexual innuendo," Rat said. "Anybody who isn't identical to James Dean in every respect tries to get fresh with me, he dies. But I do want you guys to spend the night in my soundproof room."

"Why?" I asked.

"To see if the werewolf comes back," Rat said, "and grab him or scare him away, or protect me from him. I haven't mentioned this before, but I don't think this was the first time he's been near my house."

"Two pizzas," Winston said.

"I beg your pardon," Rat said.

"Two Pete's Pizzas—special super size with double everything, or you sleep alone," Winston said.

"I intend to sleep alone anyway," Rat said, "in my bedroom, as you suggested."

"You want the two of us to wait in your soundproof room for the werewolf to show up?" I asked.

"And a cheesecake," Winston said, "the large size with blueberries. If you expect us to wait up all night for some werewolf, we've got to have something to snack on."

"Wait a minute," I said.

"Shut up," Winston said. "And we can play your hi-fi."

"Nobody touches my hi-fi," Rat said.

"So forget it," Winston said.

"Right," I said.

"You'll handle the records by the edges?" Rat asked.

"What do you take me for?" Winston responded.

"And you won't fiddle with the needle?"

"Hey," I said.

"Is it a deal or not?" Winston asked.

"Deal," Rat said.

"What?" I said.

Hail to thee writhe spirit!
Bitten thou never wert—

No more alone. I will have a friend. There will be another to cavort beneath the moon. A nip, a nibble, a little bite, snap! A flower of a special kind presented in the light of the moon.

And then . . .

And then . . .

A transformation, a realization! I will wait. I will wait. I will put the bite on this one.

And then . . .

And then . . .

She will be like me!

The Honorable Lama Lumpo Smythe-Finkel sits in meditation in an upstairs room in his suburban yurt. He chants the ancient chants, counts his breaths, turns his eyes inward. He holds his hands in a complicated gesture, the mudra of the venerable Serious Hat sect. As he sits, the material universe recedes. An invisible galaxy revolves around him. His body is suffused with light. He levitates slightly, hovering an inch above the carpet.

It is an ordinary session, such as he has every night after watching the rerun of *Mary Tyler Moore.*

This time something unforeseen, something unimagined, something amazing happens.

From the ceiling of the room in which he sits there falls into his arms, outstretched in the posture of supplication, a book! A real book!

It is exactly the size and weight and shape of *Kenkyusha's Japanese-English Dictionary*—but it is another book.

The lama looks at the book in amazement. In over two years of meditating, nothing like this has ever happened.

He reads the title, stamped in finest gold on the front cover:

The Lycanthropicon

He opens the book. He reads.

"Oh my!" the lama says aloud. "Oh my goodness! Oh!"

The book dematerializes. It is suddenly thin air. It is no more.

"Oh my!" the lama says. "Oh! Oh boy! Oh! Oh! Wow!"

He rushes downstairs to use the telephone.

Rat has one of the finest record collections I've ever seen. Under ordinary circumstances I would have been delighted to have a whole night with Winston, two giant pizzas, and a cheesecake in her soundproof room. When you listen to records with Rat, it is very much her choice as to what will be played. There were records in her collection which we had heard only once—or only heard snatches of. Staying all night and watching for the werewolf provided Winston and me with a chance to hear whatever we wanted.

On the other hand, I had a hard time really enjoying myself. I kept thinking about the fact that should the werewolf show up, there was no way to summon help. We could holler our heads off in that room, and nobody would hear a thing. We'd phoned home to say that we were staying over at Rat's house. There was no problem with our respective parents—although it felt funny to us to be making an excuse for staying away from home all night that wasn't a lie. We didn't say anything about waiting up for a werewolf—it was really none of their business.

The first thing Winston wanted to do was eat a lot. Once that was taken care of, he selected some records he wanted to play. I myself didn't have any preference. I was worried about what would happen if the werewolf showed up.

The first record that Winston played was one of Lord Buckley. Lord Buckley is one of the most revolutionary and amazing people ever to live. Rat had once played us a single cut from her Lord Buckley record. It knocked us out. Lord Buckley was this hipster back sometime in history—maybe the 1950s or '60's. He was like a comedian, but what he did was also like jazz.

Listening to Lord Buckley straightened my wig—that is, I got a lot calmer about the likelihood of a werewolf turning up, and I even got involved with the pizza. Winston's next choice was a record of blues by Blind Lemon—also great. Then we listened to *Don Giovanni* by Mozart. Winston has eclectic tastes.

At one point I thought I heard a scratching at the door. Except for that, nothing happened. When Rat came to check on us in the morning, we were in a good mood and ready to have breakfast with Rat's family.

While Winston Bongo and Walter Galt were sitting up all night in Rat's soundproof room, eating giant pizzas and cheesecake and listening to records—while Rat was sleeping in her bed—while all the city was quiet—a strange meeting was taking place in a nearly deserted all-night diner on the edge of town.

The Honorable Lama Lumpo Smythe-Finkel, the bookseller Howling Frog, and another man, who kept the collar of his coat turned up, and the brim of his hat turned down, sat at a booth at the far end of the Deadly Nightshade Diner—We Never Close. The men spoke in hushed tones and consumed plates of french fries with catsup.

If one had been sitting in the booth next to the one occupied by the three men (which no one was) one might have heard a whispered word or two. If one had been situated inside the napkin dispenser on the table (which no one could have been) one might have heard the Honorable Lama Lumpo Smythe-Finkel speak these words:

"In all my two years as a mystic lama and meditator, nothing this amazing has ever happened to me. It is as though I had been singled out, chosen from among all mankind to receive this vital information."

If one were a spoon on the table (which no one could possibly be), or if a spoon were a sensate thing with ears and a mind (which spoons are not), one might have heard the bookseller, Howling Frog, say:

"If the lama's information, which is of the nature of a mystical revelation, is true, the situation is one of great seriousness and danger. We thought it best to consult with you at once."

If one were the coat collar of the stranger with the slouch hat (which would be utterly ridiculous) one might, with great difficulty, have heard him say in the lowest possible whisper:

"Yes, yes, you acted correctly. I only hope it is not too late."

"Do you think it is possible that it is too late?" asks the bookseller in a voice so low that even the spoon can hardly hear him.

"What are you going to do?" asks the lama in an urgent whisper.

"You know my methods," says the stranger, more to his coat collar than to his companions. "I prefer not to reveal anything until I have more facts at my disposal."

"But you will help in this matter. . . ?" says the lama.

"I would be a swine not to," says the stranger.

Lydia LaZonga showed up. Rat called us to say that K.E. Kelman's mother was on her way over. We arrived two minutes before she did.

Heinz, the butler, let her in. She was about four feet tall, sort of fat, and wore a flowered print dress.

"Sonny tells me you're having a problem, dearie," Lydia LaZonga said. "Is it a hoodoo?"

"It's a werewolf," Rat said.

"Is that all? I thought it was something really complicated. Ordinarily this is my day to go marketing—if I'd known it was only a werewolf I wouldn't have called in such a hurry. Still, as long as I'm here . . . which one of you is the werewolf?"

"It isn't any of us," Rat said, "it's just this werewolf . . . at least I'm pretty sure it's a werewolf. I sort of saw it. It was in my room."

"I'll require a root beer, dearie," Lydia LaZonga said.

Rat sent Heinz to get a root beer for Kelman's mother. He brought it on a tray.

"I'll just take a sip of this," Lydia LaZonga said, "and we'll get to work."

Lydia LaZonga sipped her root beer. "I'm going to go into a trance now," she said. "Don't be frightened."

This was all taking place in Rat's soundproof room. That was a good thing, it turned out, because Lydia LaZonga gave out with a howl that would have scared the whole neighborhood. Then she began running around the room at top speed, hooting and yowling and waving her arms. After she did that for five or six minutes, she stood stock still, vibrated for a while, spun around three or four times, jumped straight up in the air, and collapsed on the floor.

It was a good thing Lydia LaZonga had warned us not to be frightened—not that we weren't frightened. For a second I was afraid the old lady had dropped dead.

"That was a good one," Lydia LaZonga said, "and I'm glad I came. This is a much more interesting case than I first thought."

"Is my room werewolf-proof now?" Rat asked.

"Of course, dearie," Lydia LaZonga said, "but I don't think it's going to do you much good."

"Why not?" Rat asked.

"Because I don't think there's been a real werewolf here," the hoodoo lady said.

"No?"

"No. Oh, something has been here, all right—and I suppose someone without any real experience might think it was a werewolf—but I don't feel any real werewolf vibrations."

"What do you feel?"

"Something extremely strange and evil," Lydia LaZonga said. "It isn't any of the usual kinds of haunts—I know all about those. It isn't a hoodoo, or a poltergeist, or a banshee, or a ghost, or any of the things one ordinarily encounters. The signal I'm picking up is of a human being—but not just any human being. This would be some sort of malevolent genius. Whoever this is must be the veritable Napoleon of Crime."

Winston, Rat, and I looked at each other. Wallace Nussbaum! Wallace Nussbaum, the Napoleon of

Crime, was the one who had kidnapped Rat's Uncle Flipping that time. As far as we knew he was in prison—but Lydia LaZonga's description fit him perfectly. Could she mean Nussbaum? Had she somehow picked up some sort of psychic signal from the smartest, meanest, trickiest criminal genius on earth?

"Yes, I would say it was a sort of master criminal. Understand that this very brilliant criminal is *not* the one who was here—and someone or something *was* definitely here. It's strange, but I'm getting pictures of an orangutan specially trained for evil purposes, and somebody's uncle having been kidnapped—does any of that make sense to any of you?"

It made sense. Wallace Nussbaum had used stolen orangutans trained to do his bidding as henchmen—and he had kidnapped Rat's Uncle Flipping, of course.

"What was here, I cannot say. It was like a werewolf—but it was not a werewolf. Werewolves are really good at heart—Sonny is quite fond of them, you know. The psychic emanations I'm getting are closer to those of a zombie—very rare in these parts—but it isn't a zombie either. Oh, it's very unusual. I'm glad I came. And then there's the sense of that very evil, very bright person. What he has to do with all of this, I don't know. Yes, it's a wonderful case. Well, goodbye now. I'm happy to have met you nice young people."

"That's all? You're just going?" Rat asked.

"For the present," Lydia LaZonga said, "there's nothing more for me to do here, dearie."

"So it's not a werewolf—but it's like a werewolf—it's more like a zombie, but it isn't a zombie."

"That's right, dearie. Goodbye."

And Lydia LaZonga was gone.

Is it possible that the master criminal Wallace Nussbaum is somehow involved in all this?

Anything is possible.

"I'm really confused," Rat said. "If Lydia LaZonga is anything but a fake or a looney, then what turned up here is something other than a werewolf (which I never believed in anyhow until just lately). She says it's sort of like a zombie. I don't know that much about zombies, but on the whole, I think I'd prefer a werewolf. On top of all that, she says she thinks a super criminal is involved. The only one I know about is Wallace Nussbaum."

Winston spoke. "Isn't Wallace Nussbaum still in jail?"

"As far as I know, he is," Rat said. "They reopened Devil's Island just for him."

"Well, then, it can't be Wallace Nussbaum," I said. "It's impossible to escape from Devil's Island."

SUPER-CRIMINAL WALLACE NUSSBAUM HAS AP-
PARENTLY ESCAPED FROM DEVIL'S ISLAND. IT WAS BE-
LIEVED THAT THE FORMER FRENCH PENAL COLONY,
CLOSED IN THE LATE 1940'S AND REOPENED FOR THE
EXPRESS PURPOSE OF IMPRISONING NUSSBAUM, WAS ES-
CAPE-PROOF—HOWEVER, THERE IS NO SIGN OF THE ONE
AND ONLY INMATE. THE ONE HUNDRED AND FORTY-ONE
GUARDS HAVE SEARCHED THE ISLAND THREE TIMES, AND
REPORT THAT NUSSBAUM CANNOT BE FOUND.

IN A STATEMENT TO THE PRESS, CAPTAIN DE BOLDIEU,
COMMANDANT OF THE PRISON, SAID, "I SUPPOSE IT IS TOO
MUCH TO HOPE THAT A SHARK HAS EATEN THE TERRIBLE
FELLOW. NO, I THINK HE HAS GOTTEN CLEAN AWAY. I FEEL
SO SILLY."

LAW ENFORCEMENT OFFICIALS THE WORLD OVER
HAVE ECHOED THE SENTIMENTS OF THE SILLY FRENCH-
MAN. IT SEEMS MOST LIKELY THAT NUSSBAUM HAS
ESCAPED ONCE MORE, AND A WORLDWIDE CRIME WAVE IS
EXPECTED.

IN THE LOCAL NEWS, THE BACONBURG HORROR HAS
STRUCK AGAIN. EXTENSIVE DAMAGE WAS DONE TO THE
PAVEMENT OUTSIDE BACONBURG CITY HALL. THE SIDE-
WALK HAS BEEN RIPPED UP ALL ALONG ONE SIDE OF NIBITZ
STREET. TOOTHMARKS ARE CLEARLY DISCERNIBLE IN THE
CONCRETE. THERE IS CONSIDERABLE PANIC AMONG THE
CITIZENS. MAYOR BEESLEY IS VACATIONING IN THE BA-
HAMAS, AND WAS UNAVAILABLE FOR COMMENT.

Lydia LaZonga is speaking on the telephone: "Sonny, I have to talk to you right away. Meet me at the Deadly Nightshade Diner—We Never Close in one hour."

The Honorable Lama Lumpo Smythe-Finkel is speaking on the telephone: "Frog, I've thought more about what I told you—and the other one. Let's meet again at the Deadly Nightshade Diner—We Never Close—say, in one hour?"

Jonathan Quicksilver, the avant-garde poet, felt hungry. He had been preoccupied with worry that jealous fellow poets were circulating werewolf rumors to keep his audiences small at the Dharma Buns Coffee House. For days he had eaten nothing but horrible doughnuts. Thinking that perhaps some superior nutrition might help him work up a poem or two, he left his room on the edge of town and headed for the nearest diner.

"Look, we're letting this get to us," Winston said. "What we need is some recreation. Let's go for a spin in the car—maybe we'll wind up at a diner or something."

The world's greatest detective whacked his Dunhill against the heel of his shoe. "Now, Doctor," he said to his companion, "I think a brisk walk to the Deadly Nightshade Diner—We Never Close will do us both good. What's more, I feel a bit peckish, and could do with a serving of their excellent raisin toast."

Scott Feldman and his father, Phelps Feldman, are on their way home. Mr. Feldman has picked up his son at the dancing academy where young Scott is taking samba lessons. They decide to drop in at the Deadly Nightshade Diner—We Never Close for some tapioca pudding and Postum.

I stalk the streets. I run and jump. I howl and yell.
I ... where is everybody?

It is an age long past. A time before our grandfathers' time. In a capital of eastern Europe a level of elegance and grace exists, unknown to dwellers in western lands. Dashing officers and graceful ladies dance the *hüpisch*. Gleaming horses draw elegant carriages. Everywhere is heard the clink of glasses and the cry *"Wupski!"* as the genteel and decorous citizens celebrate the carrot-wine vintage. Scholars and artists collide in the streets. Trade prospers. Culture flourishes. Time stands still.

It is within this happy, carefree moment in history that the first recorded ancestor of an illustrious family descends from a remote mountain village to seek his fortune in the great city. Hubertus Baolungpinski, a self-taught chef and genius, opens a modest eating house, the Transylvanian Mushroom—We Never Close. Baolungpinski works hard, and soon becomes a celebrated restaurateur, famous for his foot-long borgelnuskies.

Generations later, a proud tradition continues. On the edge of the city of Baconburg, a descendant of the first Baolungpinski, Gus Bowlingpin, operates an establishment cherished by gourmets, the Deadly Nightshade Diner—We Never Close.

Unprepossessing, simple, a bit filthy, this great restaurant caters to a clientele which knows that a really superior rice pudding is worth enduring a little inconvenience—and is not stampeded by the germ theory and other unworthy ideas of a corrupt and cynical age.

It is here, among old-world surroundings and the sights and smells associated with great food, that the elite of Baconburg gather to enjoy raisin toast, California cheeseburgers, and the spécialité de la maison, the jitterbug—a scoop of creamy mashed potato atop a slice of magnificent meatloaf—not too hot and not too cold—beneath which is a slice of fresh and nutritious Wonder bread, all of this deliciousness topped with yummy brown gravy—a dish fit for the most discerning palate.

It is a busy evening at the Deadly Nightshade Diner—We Never Close. In the booths patrons converse in cultured tones.

"I tell you, Frog—and Mr. Sigerson—this has me very worried. Why was I selected to receive this amazing information? What can it mean? Who is this evil person? What can we do?" It is the Honorable Lama Lumpo Smythe-Finkel speaking to his friend the bookseller Howling Frog, and to Osgood Sigerson, the world's greatest private detective. Another man is present, Dr. Ormond Sacker, Sigerson's companion and biographer.

Osgood Sigerson speaks: "I am not one to doubt the events which befall the faithful. I believe that a book—or something which you took to be a book—fell from the ceiling during your meditation. As to the message you read in that miraculous book, I have given it much thought. Just tell my friend Dr. Sacker what you read."

"Gladly," says the lama. "It was in the form of a

poem. It was unclear to me what the meaning was—but I had a feeling of unutterable horror when I read the words. They were these:

> *"A man who is a wolf—*
> *A wolf who is a man—*
> *Revealed thus is the meaning of this rhyme.*
> *It is not a wolfman, nor a manwolf—*
> *Not as such—*
> *It's the work of the Napoleon of Crime."*

"Amazing, Sigerson!" Dr. Sacker exclaims. "The meaning is perfectly clear—and, may I say, it makes my skin crawl!"

"And what do you take the meaning to be, old fellow?" the great detective asks.

"Why, there is some terrible crime afoot which involves fine pastry—namely Napoleons!" says the good doctor.

"You are improving, old chap," says Sigerson. "That is exactly the meaning I give the poem. Good for you!"

"Yes, but I was thinking," says the lama, "couldn't the phrase 'Napoleon of Crime,' pertain to a person—say a person who was an outstanding criminal? You know, one might say 'the Einstein of Crime,' or 'the Leonardo da Vinci of Crime,' meaning a major criminal genius."

"Ah, Lama," says Sigerson, "it is best to leave these things to the professional criminologist—still, your idea is not without merit. It is rather intriguing—but . . . no, I hardly think so—I mean, a pastry is hardly the same thing as Einstein or Leonardo da Vinci, is it? I mean, to say that one is 'the pastry of crime,' it's rather ridiculous, what?"

"I was thinking of Bonaparte," says the lama.

"Of which?"

"Of Napoleon Bonaparte—thought by many to have been the greatest man in Europe at one time—not the pastry—the emperor of France," the lama explains.

"Oh," says the great detective. "Of course. Ah. Hum. Mmm. Hmmm. I'll have to smoke my pipe and think about this for a while."

In another booth, another conversation:

"Sonny," Lydia Kelman, also known as Lydia La-Zonga, says to her son, K.E. Kelman, PH., "this is a very unusual case. My psychic powers tell me that we are not dealing with a werewolf—which is old hat for both of us—but some kind of evil genius. I'm afraid he means to do some harm."

"Mommy, are you going to finish that seven-layer cake?" asks the phantomologist.

"I'm afraid those nice children may be in some sort of danger," says Lydia LaZonga, "and yes, I am going to finish my cake—I'm just resting."

In another booth:

"This is good tapioca pudding, isn't it, Daddy?"

"It certainly is, son. I always say there's nothing like tapioca pudding late at night to make one feel tickety-poo."

"I'm making progress in my samba lessons."

"That's excellent, son."

In another booth, Jonathan Quicksilver, the poet, writes on a napkin:

```
THAT WEREWOLF              BOY

          IT

       REALLY

        BUGS

         ME

      I KNOW

   THAT    IT

          HAS SOMETHING AGAINST

               ME

      PERSONALLY


         WOW
              *
```

In another booth:

"So then James Dean says to Hitler, 'I'm going to wipe the floor with you,' and Hitler says, 'Ach, you sniveling degenerate amerikanischer film actor—mit one hand tied behind my back, I can make wiener schnitzel of you,' and then James Dean says ... Heinz!"

Heinz, the butler, has appeared in the Deadly Nightshade Diner—We Never Close. "Miss Rat," says Heinz, "I am sorry to disturb you with your friends, but your Uncle Flipping requests that you come home at once. He says it is something important. I have brought the car."

Rat departs with Heinz, leaving Walter Galt and Winston Bongo alone in the booth. "She sure loves James Dean," Walter says.

"By Jove! You're right, Lama!" the great detective

shouts. "How could I have been so blind! It is not the Napoleon of Crime, meaning the pastry of crime—it is the Napoleon of Crime, meaning the world's nastiest and most brilliant criminal! Wallace Nussbaum!"

"I'm getting a psychic wave," says Lydia LaZonga. "A name is coming to me. I can see it plainly—it is . . . Wallace Nussbaum."

"Say, Walter," Winston Bongo says, "remember when Uncle Flipping was kidnapped that time?"

"Sure," says Walter Galt.

"Well, when we found him and rescued him from Wallace Nussbaum, the master criminal, didn't Nussbaum turn out to actually be—"

"Heinz the butler!" Walter shouts.

"And Nussbaum is supposedly on Devil's Island, but just a few minutes ago, Heinz was in here."

"That is funny, isn't it?"

"Rat never said anything—and her family never said anything. You don't suppose they'd allow Heinz to be around, knowing that he was Nussbaum?"

"It wouldn't make sense."

"It must be something we missed."

"You mean Heinz's twin, or something like that."

"Yes, something like that."

"Must be."

"Funny though."

"I really like tapioca pudding, Daddy."

"So do I, son."

"REALLY   BUGS   ME   WOW"

"Sacker, if ever I seem to grow too sure of myself—if ever I am too cocky—too smartypants—just whisper one word in my ear."

"What word is that, Sigerson?"

"Nussbaum—or Napoleon—or better, Lama—no, Nussbaum is better—whisper Nussbaum."

"You want me to whisper Nussbaum?"

"That's right."

"Nussbaum."

"No, not now, you idiot—when I'm too cocky, whisper Nussbaum."

"Not now?"

"No—wait until I am too sure of myself—*then* whisper Nussbaum."

"How will I know?"

"Know what?"

"When you want me to whisper Nussbaum."

"It's not when I want you to whisper Nussbaum—it's when I'm getting too sure of myself—then you whisper Nussbaum to remind me of what a fool I was about the message in the lama's book."

"Nussbaum."

"No! Not now!"

"On the other hand, Rat's family is pretty crazy."

"That's true."

"If by some chance the Heinz who was just in here is the same Heinz they've always had."

"Then he would be Nussbaum."

"Unless we missed something."

"You know," Howling Frog said, "we ought to come back here on Thursday. That's when they have borgelnuskies."

"No fooling, the foot-long ones?" asked Osgood Sigerson, the world's greatest detective.

"The very best," said the bookseller.

"But what does this Wallace Nussbaum, this Napoleon of Crime—meaning Napoleon Bonaparte, not the pastry—have to do with the werewolf?" the Honorable Lama Lumpo Smythe-Finkel asked.

"I like borgelnuskies with cole slaw and lots of mustard," said Dr. Ormond Sacker, the friend and biographer of the great sleuth.

"So do I," said Sigerson, "and grilled onions—what was that you said, Lama?"

"I was wondering what the criminal genius had to do with a werewolf."

"Who says he has anything to do with a werewolf?" asked the detective. "And root beer—you can't have borgelnuskies without root beer by the pitcher."

"It's in the poem—the poem that was revealed to me in the book—you remember:

"A man who is a wolf—
A wolf who is a man—"

"Ah, yes," said Osgood Sigerson:

> *"It is not a wolfman, nor a manwolf—*
> *Not as such—*
> *It's the work of the Napoleon of Crime.*

"It still makes me think of the pastry—although I have no doubt that the Nussbaum interpretation is the correct one. What was the question?"

"What is the connection?" asked the lama, speaking slowly. "The connection between the master criminal and the werewolf?"

"Ah, well, that is what we have to find out, isn't it, Lama? That is where I come in. That is where I get to use my unusual powers of reasoning, isn't it? That's where all the fun starts."

"You have a suspicion, Sigerson?" asked Dr. Sacker.

"You know my methods, Sacker," the detective replied. "I prefer to remain silent until I have something conclusive with which to amaze you. There's no chance of getting a borgelnuskie today, do you suppose, Frog?"

"No, he only makes them on Thursdays."

"Pity."

"Look," said Walter Galt, "isn't that Osgood Sigerson sitting over there with Howling Frog and the Honorable Lama Lumpo Smythe-Finkel?"

"It is," said Winston Bongo. "We haven't seen him since we helped him solve the disappearance of Rat's Uncle Flipping."

"Let's go over and say hello."

The two boys approached the booth in which the

great detective was sitting. "Mr. Sigerson, do you remember us?" said Walter.

"I should say I do!" replied the detective. "It's Larry and Jerry, the Bloomsbury Burglars. Still at large, but not for long. Dr. Sacker, I trust you have your weapon with you. Hands up, the two of you—Dr. Sacker has you covered with an Indian fruit bat. I must say I like your nerve—walking right up to me like this. I'll just put the darbies on you and march you to the police station. Put out your wrists. This is a good night's work indeed."

"We're not burglars," Winston said. "We're Winston Bongo and Walter Galt. We helped you rescue Flipping Hades Terwilliger the time he was kidnapped by Wallace Nussbaum."

"These confounded bifocals," said Osgood Sigerson. "Of course you are. You know, you look exactly like a couple of burglars. Come join us. Doctor, slide over and make some room for these two fine young men. Do you boys come here often? Have you ever eaten the borgelnuskies?"

"We have them all the time," Winston said.

"Really? Any good?" asked Sigerson.

"I like them," said Winston.

"Well, we'll have to come back on Thursday, and that's that," said Sigerson. "You remember my colleague, Dr. Sacker—and these gentlemen are . . ."

"We've already met," said Howling Frog. "And how is Miss Rat, your young lady friend?"

"She was here a little while ago," Walter said. "She left with her butler, Heinz—in fact, there was a question we were discussing which you might help us with, Mr. Sigerson."

"I'm always happy to make things clear for the young."

"Well, when we caught Nussbaum that time . . ."

Howling Frog and the lama exchanged surprised glances.

". . . didn't it turn out that he was actually Heinz the butler?"

"I lose track of details once a case is finished," said Sigerson. "Doctor, what do you recall of the matter?"

"Yes," Dr. Sacker said. "I seem to remember that Nussbaum was masquerading as the family butler."

"Well, Heinz has been around ever since, just as if nothing had happened. Everybody in Rat's family seemed so unconcerned that we just never gave it a thought. We assumed that it was Heinz's twin or something—besides, Wallace Nussbaum went to Devil's Island, from which nobody has ever escaped. But we were just wondering what the story was."

A voice from the next booth was raised in a mournful wail, "But Wallace Nussbaum *has* escaped from Devil's Island. It was in the paper this morning!" It was the poet Jonathan Quicksilver who spoke.

"This is the poet Jonathan Quicksilver," Winston said. "Quicksilver, this is Osgood Sigerson, the world's greatest detective, and his friend and biographer, Dr. Ormond Sacker, and this is Howling Frog the bookseller—and I believe you know the Honorable Lama Lumpo Smythe-Finkel."

"Guru!" said Quicksilver.

"My son," said the lama, patting Quicksilver on the head.

"Squeeze over and make some room for the poet,"

said Sigerson. "Now, what did you say about Nussbaum escaping from Devil's Island?"

"It was in the *Baconburg Free Press* this morning," the poet said. "He got away and didn't leave a trace. I'm considering writing a poem about it."

"This gets more interesting by the minute," said Sigerson.

"But what does it have to do with a werewolf?" asked the lama.

"I'll tell you what it has to do with a werewolf," someone said. Standing by the booth was Lydia LaZonga Kellman, and her son, K.E. Kelman, PH.

Walter did the honors. "Lydia LaZonga Kelman and K.E. Kelman, PH., this is Osgood Sigerson, Dr. Ormond Sacker, his friend and biographer, the Honorable Lama Lumpo Smythe-Finkel, Jonathan Quicksilver, and Howling Frog."

"We've met," said Howling Frog. "These good folks are customers of mine."

"Come sit down," said Sigerson. "Everybody move over and make room. Shall we order some more raisin toast?"

"You said you would tell us what Wallace Nussbaum had to do with a werewolf," said the lama.

"I will," said Lydia LaZonga. "First of all, you must understand that I am psychic."

"Who isn't?" said the lama.

"I have had a vision in connection with a werewolf investigation I recently made, and the name Wallace Nussbaum came to me."

"Most interesting," said Osgood Sigerson.

"May my father and I sit with you?" asked Scott Feldman.

"Why not?" said the world's greatest detective. "Everybody move over."

It was good and crowded in the booth. Osgood Sigerson ordered raisin toast for everybody, and a pitcher of root beer. I could hardly work an arm free to get at my food.

Lydia LaZonga was speaking. "When I visited Rat, the friend of these two boys, it was a routine job—a werewolf-proofing. What I discovered was far from routine. I got the most confusing vibrations, didn't I, Sonny?"

"Mommy was really a mess after she left that place," K.E. Kelman, PH., said, "I had to take her to the Zen Chiropractor for a treatment."

"That's right," said Lydia LaZonga Kelman. "What I received in my psychic trance was this—it isn't a real werewolf. It's like a werewolf—but it isn't a werewolf. For a little while I thought it was a zombie—but it wasn't a zombie. And I also got strong sensations relating to some sort of fiend, or master criminal. I just a little while ago received the name Wallace Nussbaum. Well, gentlemen, this is what I think: Wallace Nussbaum has taken over the mind of someone, and has turned that person into a sort of pseudo-lycanthrope. Possibly the person has no idea that he or she is acting on instructions from this Nussbaum."

"Sigerson! This is hideous!" Dr. Ormond Sacker shouted.

"It is indeed," said the great detective. "It makes

Nussbaum's unauthorized use of hypnotized orangutans seem like a harmless prank. Madam, do you believe this pseudo-werewolf has the same powers as a
real one?''

"At least," said Lydia LaZonga. "The psychic emanations I picked up indicated a very powerful presence
indeed.''

"And it's ruining my life!" moaned Jonathan
Quicksilver. "People are afraid to be in the streets after
dark, and my audiences at the Dharma Buns Coffee
House have dwindled away to almost nothing!"

"You seem very up-to-date on the subject of werewolves," said Sigerson. "How do you know so much?"

"I read a book about them," said the poet.

"I wrote that book," said K.E. Kelman, PH., "and
it's quite true, werewolves can cause a lot of trouble,
although we shouldn't blame them too much—high
spirits and all that, you know."

"I can assure you," said Lydia LaZonga, "if any
werewolf can be a source of trouble, this artificially
created one can—it's a regular monster of a werewolf."

"It is that," said someone standing in the aisle of
the Deadly Nightshade Diner—We Never Close. "My
hypno-simulated werewolf is the most energetic creature on this planet—and it is just in the testing stage.
Wait until I have made some improvements and have
turned a few hundred thousand of them loose. Things
will be very amusing, I promise you."

"Who is that man, Daddy?" Scott Feldman asked.

We all looked at the person who was speaking.
"Heinz!" Winston shouted.

"Not Heinz. Heinz, my bionic accomplice, is

guarding my hostage—your friend Rat. I am Wallace Nussbaum. . . . Ah, ah, ah! Dr. Sacker, I know you have an Indian fruit bat at the ready beneath the table—but I caution you to take a moment's thought. My Heinz android has instructions to do something really unpleasant to Miss Rat if I do not emerge from this diner in five minutes."

"Remain calm, Sacker," Osgood Sigerson said, "Nussbaum has us where he wants us. Nussbaum, I warn you, release the girl or I will have vengeance— you know I mean what I say."

"Miss Rat will be released unharmed, Sigerson—if I am permitted to leave this place, and none of you try to follow me; otherwise it will just be too bad. I only wanted to come here and taunt you in person, you silly detective. I have escaped from Devil's Island. I have been harassing this city with a lycanthrope of my own making since even before I escaped. And I am going to create many more such werewolves now that I am free, and dominate the world—and there isn't a single thing you can do about it, Sigerson. Now, how does that make you feel—pretty frustrated, I'll bet. *Nyah na na nyah nyah!*" Nussbaum thumbed his nose at Osgood Sigerson.

"You may taunt me all you like, Nussbaum . . ."

"Thanks, I will." Nussbaum stuck out his tongue and made rude gestures at Sigerson.

". . . but you will never prosper in your evil plans." Osgood Sigerson was obviously furious, but spoke in calm and measured tones.

"We'll see about that, Mr. World's Greatest Detective," the evil Nussbaum said. "Now I'm going—and remember what I said. If any of you follow me, Rat's head will be about the size of a Ping-Pong ball in less time than it takes to tell."

Nussbaum was gone. "Quick, Sigerson! Follow him!" Dr. Ormond Sacker shouted.

"No, old fellow. You heard his threats—I believe he would carry them out. We will just sit here and finish our raisin toast."

"But, Sigerson!"

"Not to worry. Our old friend the Mighty Gorilla—the uncle of Winston here—is lurking in the shadows with instructions from me."

Outside the Deadly Nightshade Diner—We Never Close, the Mighty Gorilla, professional wrestler, crouched in the bushes and watched. He watched Heinz, the butler, emerge from the diner with Rat, and drive off in the direction of Rat's home. He watched Wallace Nussbaum emerge from a sleek limousine and enter the diner. He watched Wallace Nussbaum emerge from the diner and speed away in the limousine, apparently driven by a large ape.

And, while the Mighty Gorilla watched, someone—or something—watched him.

They are in the diner. I am outside. One crouches in the bushes. I crouch too. He is big. He watches. One comes out. It is Rat. My favorite. Her butler is with her. They go. My master comes. He goes in. I watch. The big one watches. My master comes out. He goes. The big one watches. I watch too.

"What is Scott Feldman doing here?" I thought to myself.

"This is exciting," Scott Feldman said.

"It sure is," said Phelps Feldman, his father, "and this is good raisin toast too."

"What wimps," I thought.

"Sigerson," Dr. Sacker said, "do you think that fiend will keep his word and release Rat?"

"I think Miss Rat is not in the slightest danger," Osgood Sigerson said.

"You do?"

"Elementary, my dear Sacker. Just take this dime, young Mr. Bongo, and telephone your friend Rat at her home."

"Do you think she'll be there already?" Winston asked.

"I think she hasn't been anywhere else," Sigerson said. "When she answers, tell her that I am here, and to tell Heinz—and that I want them both to come here at once—now, who would like some french fries? I'm having some."

Winston went to the pay telephone at the end of the diner. I went with him. "Hello, may I speak to Rat, please?" he said into the receiver. Apparently Rat came to the phone in a few seconds, because he said, "Rat? Is that you? Osgood Sigerson the detective is here . . . at the Deadly Nightshade Diner—We Never Close. He wants you to tell Heinz that he's here, and then come down here with Heinz as soon as you can." He hung up the receiver and turned to me. "She's home," he said.

When we got back to the booth everybody was nibbling french fries that Osgood Sigerson had ordered. "I take it the young woman was at home?" Sigerson said.

"She's coming right down here . . . with Heinz," Winston said.

"But Sigerson, if this Heinz is really an android or robot created by Nussbaum, as he said—isn't it dangerous to have told it that you are here?"

"My dear friend, I assure you Heinz is not an android or a bionic butler. You see, androids cannot pronounce their R's or L's, and they make a buzzing noise when they try to pronounce their Z's. To place an android butler in a household wherein a person named Rat lives—and someone named Flipping— would be folly. And to name the android Heinz would be another giveaway. You boys are frequently guests in the house—have you ever noticed that Heinz addresses your friend as Llat, or her uncle as Frrriping?"

We said that we hadn't.

"So many of the parts are made in Asia, you see," said Sigerson, "it's just a little problem of pronunciation that never got worked out. Now, who wants Nesselrode pie?"

The Mighty Gorilla entered the diner.

Mrs. Starkley, Rat's English teacher, who was sitting in a booth near the entrance, took one look and fainted. Later, she would revive and ask the Mighty Gorilla for his autograph.

"Everybody squeeze over and make room for the Mighty Gorilla," Osgood Sigerson said. "Mr. Mighty Gorilla, make your report."

"I waited outside," the world-famous wrestler said. "Rat left with Heinz, the butler. They drove off in the direction of Rat's house. A little while later, Wallace Nussbaum turned up. I could have tackled him, but you told me not to reveal myself on any account."

"Quite right, too," Sigerson said. "We've a werewolf to catch—and capturing Nussbaum, dear as that thought is to my heart, is of secondary importance. Pray continue."

"In a little while, Nussbaum came out of the diner and drove off in a limousine. I couldn't tell for certain, but the driver seemed not to be human."

"An unfortunate orangutan trapped in Nussbaum's power, no doubt," Sigerson said. "And the direction in which Nussbaum drove?"

"Opposite to that taken by Rat," the Mighty Gorilla said.

"So Nussbaum was bluffing, as I thought—still, I couldn't take a chance."

"This is exciting, isn't it, Daddy?" Scott Feldman said.

"Do you mean we might have grabbed Nussbaum when he was here?" Dr. Ormond Sacker asked.

"We might have," said the great detective, "but what if he actually was holding Rat captive? Nussbaum is not above kidnapping, as Rat's Uncle Flipping knows very well. Strange that we haven't seen Flipping this night—no doubt he'll turn up before this case is over. Ah, Miss Rat! And Heinz! Make room, everybody. Kindly join us, the two of you.

"And now, let's clear up the matter of Heinz's identity. Heinz, tell these people your real name."

"My real name," said the butler, "is Nussbaum."

"No, Doctor, there's no need to go for your stuffed Indian fruit bat. Tell us your first name."

"My first name is Heinrich."

"Quite so—Heinrich Nussbaum. And you are the identical twin of . . ."

"Wallace Nussbaum."

"So there you have it. Heinz the butler is the identical twin of Wallace Nussbaum. I summoned Mr. Heinrich Nussbaum from Peru to take the place of his brother in the Matthews home when it turned out that his evil twin, Wallace Nussbaum, had been masquerading as the family butler."

"I hate my brother. He's so evil," Heinrich Nussbaum said.

"Of course you do," said Sigerson. "I desired Heinrich here to take his brother's place in order that he might keep watch over the family. Mr. Heinrich Nussbaum is a member of the Peruvian police, and is fully trained."

"It is my dearest wish to bring my evil brother to justice and to remove the terrible blot on the Nussbaum name," Heinrich Nussbaum said.

"Perfectly understandable," Sigerson said. "The family was sworn to secrecy in this matter—and was instructed to behave as if this man was the same butler they'd always had—and, identical as he is to the other Nussbaum—"

"But only in appearance," Heinrich Nussbaum put in.

"But only in appearance—the family soon more or less forgot that this was another Heinz in place of the one who had proved so disloyal to them."

"When we were young, he used to steal my girl-friends," Heinrich Nussbaum said.

"And what have you observed which might be of help to us in thwarting your brother's evil plans?" Sigerson asked.

"Well, nothing, really—but I certainly do want you to thwart him. I hope you thwart him good."

Turning to Rat, Sigerson asked, "How's your Uncle Flipping been?"

"He hasn't been around much lately," Rat said. "He's been working on a new project—he's a mad scientist, you know."

"What is the nature of this new project?" asked Sigerson.

"It's a way of programming information into foodstuffs," Rat said. "Uncle Flipping first got the idea when he absentmindedly put a tortilla into the disk drive of his computer—he was eating tacos as he worked. Uncle Flipping wondered if it might be possible to load the tortilla with information from the computer which would be released directly into the brain when the tortilla was eaten. He experimented with pizza, saltines, and pancakes. Then he made an adapted disk drive machine out of a toaster and tried whole-wheat bread, bagels, and frozen waffles.

"None of the experiments worked. Uncle Flipping also tried eating standard computer disks—and that had no effect either. He decided that he had to find an edible substance which also was able to retain magnetic information, which, in turn could be ingested directly into the brain.

"Finally Uncle Flipping discovered something which looked as though it might work—an Asian relative of the avocado that has magnetic properties. Uncle Flipping had decided that the best use for this invention—if he should ever get it to work—would be to make a breakfast cereal that would contain the contents of an entire high school textbook. So, for example, a pupil eating breakfast would ingest the contents of his or her civics textbook at a single sitting."

"And has your uncle made much progress with this project?" Osgood Sigerson asked.

"Who knows?" Rat said.

"And the plant which gave him so much hope— the Asian relative of the avocado—would the name of that plant be marifesa, by any chance?"

"Something like that," Rat said.

"Most interesting," said Sigerson.

"Sigerson! What does all this mean?" Dr. Ormond Sacker asked excitedly.

"Simply this, old fellow," the great detective replied, "we now see the connection between Nussbaum's presence in this city, the phenomenon of a werewolf, and the work of Flipping Hades Terwilliger."

"What is the connection?"

"I'm not prepared to reveal that as yet—but I will tell you this. The marifesa plant has something to do with werewolfery—I saw a movie all about it."

"That's all?" asked Dr. Sacker.

"That's all for the moment."

"But what about Terwilliger's project—his plan to make it possible for people to ingest information with their food?"

"I suppose it's a good idea. It will save time reading."

"Sigerson, it's dangerous!"

"What is? What's dangerous? Where?"

"Flipping Hades Terwilliger's plan! It's very dangerous! Suppose instead of the contents of a civics textbook—suppose some evil individual, like Wallace Nussbaum, should inject some horrible doctrine or bizarre mode of behavior into—let's say tapioca pudding. Everyone who ate the stuff would instantly become a slave—and we know how dearly Wallace Nussbaum wants to enslave the population of Earth."

134

Phelps and Scott Feldman looked at each other. "You don't suppose he'd put it into tapioca pudding?" Phelps asked.

"That's not the point!" Dr. Ormond Sacker said. "The point is that Flipping Hades Terwilliger is doing experiments which might lead to something like that."

"And they have to do with marifesa plants!" K.E. Kelman put in.

"And marifesa plants have to do with werewolfian matters," Lydia LaZonga said.

"And we're after a werewolf," said Sigerson. "It all begins to fit together, doesn't it?"

"You know," Heinrich Nussbaum said, "in the last letter I received from Mommy Nussbaum, down in Lima, she hinted that Wallace may have found a way to enslave the mind of another individual, and to cause that individual to behave like a werewolf—and in fact to be a werewolf to all intents and purposes, except that the individual is not a real werewolf—that is remains a werewolf only as long as my evil brother's influence continues. These were just hints, you understand. Mommy always brags about Wallace when she writes to me. I wonder if she brags about me when she writes to him."

"Did Mommy Nussbaum indicate how Wallace planned to do this?"

"This is all reading between the lines, you understand. If Mommy knew for certain about any of Wallace's criminal activities, she would tell me, because I am a policeman, you know. I think she may have mentioned that he intends to introduce something into the food of his victims."

"Aha!"

135

"Aha, Sigerson?" Dr. Ormond Sacker asked.

"Aha, definitely," said Osgood Sigerson. "It seems very likely that we now know how Wallace Nussbaum has gained control over the poor devil who is popularly known as the Baconburg Horror. The question to be answered now is, into what food has Nussbaum introduced the lycanthropy-causing marifesa and, of course, who is eating it?"

"I think I can be of some help," said Phelps Feldman. "I am a graduate chemist—and only last week I was reading something about the marifesa in *Avocados Today*."

"My father reads that magazine," Walter Galt said.

"The marifesa, both in its flower and in the avocado-like fruit, has a very strong and distinctive flavor—so if it were introduced into a food, that food would have to have a very strong flavor indeed to disguise its taste."

"Ooooh! Daddy is helping to solve the crime," Scott Feldman said.

"Shut up, son," Phelps Feldman said.

"Something with a very strong flavor, eh?" Sigerson said. "What would you suggest as a suitable foodstuff for the introduction of marifesa?"

"Only two things occur to me," Phelps Feldman said. "One is Chef Chow's Hot and Spicy Oil undiluted and by the glassful, and the other is . . . borgelnuskies. I should add that the essential properties of the marifesa are volatile and unstable. If indeed this Wallace Nussbaum is making a werewolf of someone by feeding them marifesa, the dose would have to be repeated every few days—or at the least every week."

"Most helpful, Mr. Feldman," Sigerson said. "So,

we have a theory that Wallace Nussbaum, possibly taking a clue from spying on the scientific work of Flipping Hades Terwilliger, may have created his werewolf by feeding someone a decoction of the plant marifesa. We further theorize that the dose would have to be sustained on a weekly basis—and still further we hypothesize that a suitable vehicle for the administration of this dose would be the delicacy borgelnuskies, which are available where in this city?"

"This is the only place that serves them," Winston said.

"And it serves them once a week!" said Sigerson. "It all fits. If we are not going in the wrong direction entirely, it would seem that our werewolf is a regular customer of the Deadly Nightshade Diner—We Never Close."

"This suggests that the management of this diner may have some connection with the crime," Dr. Ormond Sacker said. "Could they possibly be putting this devilish substance in all the borgelnuskies?"

"A possibility," Sigerson said. "I take it everyone here is an habitual borgelnuskie eater."

"Except us," Phelps Feldman said, "in our family we believe that borgelnuskies lead to shortness."

"I, of course, move from place to place, and alas, have no regular source of borgelnuskies," said the detective, "but many of you eat the borgelnuskies on Thursdays, do you not?"

"Whenever possible," K.E. Kelman said.

"And the rest of you?"

"Yes."

"And the hippermost citizens of Baconburg?"

"Yes."

"A bit of a puzzle," Osgood Sigerson mused. "Either the Nussbaumian pseudo-werewolf is the only one getting the special borgelnuskies—or he is getting them somewhere other than here—or we're barking up the wrong tree altogether. Now, Mr. Feldman, perhaps you would favor us with your opinion—what would you suggest as an antidote to the effects of the marifesa?"

"Well, as I said, the essential nature of the plant is unstable and volatile—if the dose were discontinued, my guess would be that the effects would wear off in short order."

"Yes, yes. This is quite enough for one night's work," Osgood Sigerson said. "Doctor, we have quite a bit of investigating to do. I propose that we agree to meet here again on Thursday. After enjoying a nutritious meal of borgelnuskies, we will go and catch the werewolf. What do you all say to that?"

"It won't be so easy to catch the werewolf," Jonathan Quicksilver said. "Werewolves are strong and fast and nasty."

"Catching the werewolf is no problem for Mommy and me," said K.E. Kelman, PH. "It's finding the werewolf that usually gives us the most trouble."

"Oh, I think we'll have little difficulty finding the werewolf," Osgood Sigerson said, "and once that's done, I can deal with Wallace Nussbaum."

"Good!" said Heinrich Nussbaum. "I hope you really thwart him this time."

"That is my intention," said the detective. "Now—one thing more. When we meet again let there be no mention of werewolves, of our plans, or anything that has transpired this evening—we do not

138

know who may be listening. We will simply meet for a pleasant evening's entertainment. I myself will discourse brilliantly on a number of subjects, and everyone will have a lovely time. After our meal we will all go in cars to a place I will suggest—and then, whatever happens will happen. Now, I bid you all good night."

When the meeting at the Deadly Nightshade Diner—We Never Close broke up Winston couldn't get the Peugeot started. Rat had a look under the hood and said that it needed a rare French engine part, a sort of terrycloth mitten that fitted on top of the carburetor. Winston looked depressed. Rat said she was pretty sure she had the part under her bed at home. She said she'd come back the next day and fix it for him. We got a ride with Rat and Heinz, also known as Heinrich Nussbaum.

During the ride, Heinrich told us something about the history of the Nussbaum family.

"There have been master criminals in our family from the beginning of history," Heinrich told us. "The Nussbaums were once a wandering band of barbarians, like the Vandals, and the Visigoths. Even earlier, it is believed, our ancestors were no-goods, chasing honest folks away from the carcasses of mastodons they had killed for food, and raiding peaceful Paleolithic settlements. Some people think Attila the Hun was a Nussbaum, and some of the nastier Roman emperors are supposed to have had Nussbaum blood.

"In modern times Moriarty Nussbaum was considered to have had the finest criminal mind in Europe, and Fu Man Nussbaum operated a vast network of spies, assassins, smugglers, thugs, and blackmailers the like of which the world had never seen. My father, Dennis Nussbaum, made the Old World too hot to hold him and emigrated to South America. He always liked my brother Wallace better than me.

"As far as I know, I am the first honest member of the Nussbaum clan. It was quite a blow to my mother when I became a member of the Peruvian police. I have been trying all my life to single-handedly offset the horrible record of my family."

"It must really bug you to have a brother like Wallace," I said.

"You have no idea," Heinrich Nussbaum said. "Oh, I hope he gets thwarted this time! I hope Mr. Sigerson really thwarts the dickens out of him!"

"You have a lot of confidence in Osgood Sigerson, don't you?" Rat asked.

"He is my benefactor," Heinrich Nussbaum said. "It was Osgood Sigerson who helped me to get into the police. They were reluctant to take me because of my family."

Then Heinrich Nussbaum broke out in evil-sounding laughter. "That fool Sigerson will never thwart my plans!" he hissed.

I felt a creeping horror, and confusion. It was as though Heinrich had suddenly gone mad—or as if he had been the evil Wallace Nussbaum all the time. Winston and Rat shuddered too. Then we realized that it had not been Heinrich who had spoken. It was the radio speaker. A voice identical to Heinrich's, but somehow evil and scary, was coming over the radio—which, to the best of my knowledge, had not even been turned on.

"Yes, my dear fat-headed Heinrich, this is your brother, Wallace. You may tell that pathetic detective that he couldn't thwart his old granny. I listened to his idiotic conversation over the little jukebox in the booth at the Deadly Nightshade Diner—We Never Close, and it is to laugh. The whole time you simple fools were sitting around theorizing and making your feeble plans, my werewolf was just outside. If I had wished, I could have had him run into the diner and give you all such halyatchkies as you never had in your lives. Ha ha ha ha!"

Then the car radio went silent. Rat, who was sitting in the front with Heinrich, fiddled with the knobs. It had been switched off when Wallace Nussbaum's voice had come over the speakers.

"How did he do that?" I asked.

"Halyatchkies?" Winston asked.

"Oh, I hope he doesn't give us halyatchkies," Heinrich said.

Rat had her Swiss Army knife out and was taking apart the panel which held the radio in the Matthews family limousine, a luxurious Edsel touring car. Having removed a few screws, she yanked out the radio, reached into the cavity in the dashboard, and felt around. "I've got something," she said. She pulled out a little box wrapped with black tape, with wires dangling from it. "Look," Rat said, "it's a little tape recorder. Wallace Nussbaum must have rigged it so that it would start playing when the ignition was turned on. The first part of the tape is probably blank. After a few minutes it spooled along to the place where his message was recorded. He must have thought it would scare us."

"It scared me," I said.

"That Wallace is so tricky!" Heinrich said.

"First thing tomorrow I'm going to check out the

jukebox in the booth and see if there's a microphone in it," Rat said. "Then I'm going to go over the Peugeot very carefully and see if there's another tape recorder, or maybe a bomb. Chances are that Wallace is the one who fritzed your engine."

"Good idea," Winston said, "especially about checking for a bomb."

"Don't worry about a thing," Rat said.

WHO'S THIS GUY

NUSSBAUM?

I

THOUGHT

A

WEREWOLF

WAS   BAD

ENOUGH

BUT

NOW

I

HEAR

IT'S

ALL

ABOUT

THIS

NUSSBAUM

GUY   WOW

PEOPLE   WILL   GO   TO   ANY   LENGTHS

TO

MESS

UP   A

POET

*

Rat didn't find a microphone in the jukebox. We did get into a certain amount of trouble with Gus Bowlingpin. We went to the same booth everybody had been sitting in the night before and ordered crullers and coffee, and then Rat whipped out her Swiss Army knife and had the jukebox in pieces in a matter of seconds. Gus hollered at us and was going to throw us out.

"Don't you want me to put it together again?" Rat asked.

This gave us the advantage. Gus grumbled, but let us stay and finish our crullers and coffee while Rat put the jukebox back together. "At least we know that Nussbaum was bluffing about listening in on our conversation last night," she said.

"Let's make sure there isn't a bomb in my car," Winston said.

"Even if he had listened, I don't know what he would have learned," I said. "I didn't understand half of what went on. It was mostly Sigerson spinning theories—and we have no idea what he's got planned for Thursday night."

"I have to go to the bathroom," Winston said. "You guys go ahead and start looking for the bomb in my car."

"Well, if any of Sigerson's theories were correct, and Nussbaum was listening, that would put him ahead of us," Rat said.

"If you find the bomb, just go ahead and neutralize it," Winston said. "Don't wait for me."

"What do you think Sigerson has planned for Thursday night?" I asked.

"It beats me," Rat said. "I don't know any more than you do. All he said was that we were going to meet for a meal of borgelnuskies—which, by the way, I can't stand—and then we would all go someplace. We're not supposed to talk about Nussbaum or the werewolf or any of that."

"Just knock on the men's room door after you disarm the bomb," Winston said.

From *The New York Times,* June 6th, 1983:

By William E. Geist

One night in 1933, Richard Holligshead, Jr., took a projector outside, flashed a movie on the side of a building, and sat in his car to watch it. Friends and family were very worried about Mr. Hollingshead. He next patented a ramp system allowing the occupants of a car to see a screen over a car in front of them, and on June 6 of that year he opened the world's first drive-in movie theater, the R. H. Hollingshead, Jr., Theater on Admiral Wilson Boulevard in Camden, N.J.

From *The Times of Africa,* Nairobi, May 28th, 1966

Eleven non-paying customers turned up at the Riziki Rafiki Drive-in Movie Theater on Kimenge Road last night. The occasion was the first showing of the film Born Free, which deals with Elsa the lioness and her cubs. During the presentation of the film, eleven lions from the Nairobi Game Refuge came over the wall, no doubt attracted by the growling and roaring on the sound track, and watched the film. The lions took up positions on the roofs and bonnets of cars, and stayed until the end of the performance.

From the *Baconburg Free Press*

In response to the revival of interest in monsters arising from the Baconburg Horror incidents, the Garden of Earthly Bliss Drive-in and Pizzeria on Route 9R has scheduled a Season of Horror festival. Beginning this Thursday at nightfall, the Garden of Earthly Bliss Drive-in and Pizzeria will show five different horror features every night.

An alternate tradition contends that it was not Richard Hollingshead, Jr., who first opened a drive-in theater, but a Romanian named Tesev Nussbaumscu who opened such an establishment in the town of Blint in 1893. Some historians argue that this was not a true drive-in in the modern sense of the word, as neither automobiles nor movies were known then, and the theater remained open for only one performance which consisted of Nussbaumscu and his family falling upon the curious, who had come in carts and wagons, beating them with halyatchkie sticks, and taking their money and possessions.

A Bucharest firm which opened a chain of drive-in movies throughout Eastern Europe in the 1930's was unaware of this event, and were taken by surprise when their Blint location was burned to the ground by an angry and suspicious populace—some of whom still remembered the Nussbaumscu affair.

Coincidentally, Louis Grotshkie, the head of the firm which built the ill-fated second drive-in movie theater in Blint, emigrated to the United States and, in time, opened the very finest drive-in movie ever, the Garden of Earthly Bliss Drive-in and Pizzeria in Baconburg.

Even more coincidentally, half the population of Blint also emigrated to the United States and settled in and around Baconburg.

Some believe that there is a connection between

the Blintish colony in Baconburg and the constant outbreak of fires at the Garden of Earthly Bliss Drive-in and Pizzeria. In any case, one of Mr. Grotshkie's constant concerns has been the repeated arson attempts at his theater. On two occasions the entire screen was immolated, and Grotshkie was forced to hire extra security guards and to install a state-of-the-art fire prevention system in the pizzeria/projection booth.

Following these innovations, would-be firebugs began bringing combustible materials into the drive-in and setting huge bonfires. This necessitated the installation of high-pressure fire hoses at strategic points in the parking area.

This was the state of affairs at the Garden of Earthly Bliss Drive-in and Pizzeria at the beginning of the Season of Horror film festival.

The moon is my friend. I sneak and hide. I love to howl. I love to pounce. I love to eat. I love to eat. I love to eat borgelnuskies. Borgelnuskies. Want borgelnuskies. Really hungry for borgelnuskies. Borgelnuskies. Is it Thursday? I smell them. The Deadly Nightshade Diner—We Never Close. Borgelnuskies. Yum. Get borgelnuskies. I drool.

Thursday night. It looked like everybody in Baconburg had turned up at the Deadly Nightshade Diner—We Never Close. There's always a mob scene when borgelnuskies are served. The parking lot was just about full. People were standing in line waiting to get in, and people were coming out with faces that expressed supreme contentment and pleasure mixed with nausea and gastritis. Rat, Winston, and I arrived in the Peugeot. Heinz, the butler who was, in reality, Heinrich Nussbaum, twin brother of Wallace Nussbaum the master criminal, was driving on his own in the Edsel limousine. We could smell the grilled onions two blocks away.

Osgood Sigerson was already in the diner. He had reserved a large booth which was rapidly filling up with people. Dr. Ormond Sacker was there, of course. Also Winston's uncle, the Mighty Gorilla, who did part-time bodyguard and strong-arm work for Sigerson. Phelps Feldman and his son Scott were there, eating corn flakes. K.E. Kelman, PH., the phantomologist, and his mother, Lydia LaZonga, were there. Jonathan Quicksilver, the poet, was there, and also his guru, the Honorable Lama Lumpo Smythe-Finkel and Howling Frog, the bookseller. Rat was surprised to see her English teacher, Mrs. Starkley, and a man who turned out to be Mr. Starkley sitting in the booth.

There was barely room for us to squeeze in—and Heinrich Nussbaum hadn't shown up yet.

"I've already ordered," Osgood Sigerson said, "you are all my guests. It's borgelnuskies for everybody—and don't be shy about asking for seconds. It's a party! Whoopee!" The world's greatest detective was in unusually high spirits. He was wearing his deerstalker cap, and was obviously excited and ready for action. He was bouncing up and down in his seat and annoying other patrons by blowing the paper sleeves off soda straws. If Winston or I had acted that way we'd have been thrown out.

"Look! Look! Here they come! Bring on the borgelnuskies, chef!" Gus Bowlingpin was carrying a tray crowded with platters of hot borgelnuskies. "Bon appétit!" Gus said.

"Hooray!" the great detective shouted, and "Dig in! Get them before they get you!"

The Mighty Gorilla made the least noise but ate the most borgelnuskies. It was a frightening spectacle, even though he didn't begin to have trouble breathing until the ninth helping. Even the Feldmans nibbled a borgelnuskie apiece, although they expressed fear that they might have indigestion later.

"Nonsense," Dr. Ormond Sacker said. "I am a medical man, and I can tell you for certain that there is no reason to worry. You *will* have indigestion later. It's the price you pay—but there's no cause for alarm. No one is apt to die from eating borgelnuskies—except perhaps the Mighty Gorilla."

"Ah!" Osgood Sigerson said. "Is it not my old friend, Flipping Hades Terwilliger?"

"Sigerson!" said Rat's uncle. "And everybody else! What a pleasure!"

"Join us," Sigerson said. "We're just having some borgelnuskies."

"Exactly what I came for," Flipping Hades Terwilliger said, "I'll just instruct the chef. Gus—a triple order of borgelnuskies, if you please, and topped with confectioner's sugar, pineapple slices, and instant-whip as usual!"

"Yich!" the Mighty Gorilla said. "Speaking as a confirmed gourmand and pig-out artist, that is the most awful-sounding combination I've ever heard of. Even I could never eat that—nobody could."

"It's the way I like them," Uncle Flipping said, "and, as I understand matters, one of the benefits of living in a democracy is that a man may eat his borgelnuskies any way he likes."

"But not in front of children!" Lydia LaZonga said.

"It's all right," Rat said, "he's my uncle."

"You poor dear," Lydia LaZonga said.

"I say, Sigerson," Dr. Ormond Sacker said. "Do you notice anything odd about that kitchen helper?"

"Yes," Osgood Sigerson said, "I've been observing the poor devil for some time—but let's not discuss such matters for the moment."

I caught a glimpse of the kitchen helper they must have been talking about. He was a poor devil if I'd ever seen one—stoop-shouldered, flat-footed, and hairy as an ape. A really ugly guy.

"I say!" Sigerson shouted. "I've been neglecting my promise to entertain you all with some brilliant conversation. Now, who here knows why tennis balls are fuzzy when they're new?"

Sigerson astounded us with obscure information for the next hour or so. "I wonder if anyone here knows how many varieties of salami there are throughout the world?" the world's greatest detective asked. "There are over a thousand! One thousand six hundred thirty-three, to be exact! Salami is one of the most ancient foodstuffs—probably originating when the first caveman, unable to finish his meal of ptero-dactyl cutlets, shoved the leftovers into a bag and then forgot about it for a month or two. I include in the general category of salami such delicacies as Chinese lop cheong and Bavarian jaegerwurst, as well as the more readily recognized varieties such as the kosher gut buster and the Hungarian black beauty."

Sigerson certainly knew a lot. From salamis, he went on to tell about the history of cuckoo clocks, favorite footwear of the pre-Socratic philosophers, and whether there is life on other planets. Cuckoo clocks were first made in Turkey, not Switzerland, most of the pre-Socratic philosophers liked open-toed sandals, and in Sigerson's opinion, beings from other planets not only exist, but visit Earth regularly. It isn't often that one gets to listen to a really brilliant person. I was impressed.

While Sigerson talked he munched borgelnuskies. The rest of us ate quite a few too. We all began to feel quite full—which, when you've been eating borgel-nuskies, is what you feel just before the pain begins. Sigerson interrupted himself in the middle of an inter-esting account of the different varieties of African zebras and said, "I say! Who's for a movie?"

For myself, I was more in the mood to go home and writhe on my bed until the effects of eating borgelnus-kies had worn off. I would have thought the others felt the same way, but Dr. Ormond Sacker said, "By Jove! What a capital idea! What precisely did you have in mind, Sigerson?"

"I believe we have the honor to have among us

three—no, four of the greatest exponents of the art of snarking," Sigerson said. "I refer, of course, to young Rat, Walter, and Winston, and the distinguished scientist Flipping Hades Terwilliger. May I make so bold to suggest that they lead us all on a grand mechanized outdoor snark?"

"A grand mechanized outdoor snark?" Winston asked.

"Precisely," Sigerson said. "With such a large group of distinguished persons, it seems to me that the ordinary sort of snark might call upon us for less than our best effort. What I propose is that we all get in cars, and just go."

"Go?" the Honorable Lama Lumpo Smythe-Finkel asked. "Go where?"

"I thought it would be fun if you all didn't know exactly where quite yet," Osgood Sigerson said. "We will all get into cars and begin driving. Before that, I will give you sealed envelopes—one envelope to each car. Once we are all rolling, someone in each car will open the envelope. Inside the envelope will be instructions for our snark. It's something like a treasure hunt or a game. Doesn't it sound like fun? Now, who wants to go?"

Everybody wanted to go except Uncle Flipping. Uncle Flipping said he had some work to finish at his laboratory—but if Sigerson would give him one of the sealed envelopes, he would try to catch up with us later.

"That will be no problem at all," Osgood Sigerson said. "Here is your envelope. Now, shall we all get started?"

157

It was Rat, Winston, and me in the Peugeot. Osgood Sigerson and Dr. Ormond Sacker went with the Mighty Gorilla in their famous Studebaker Lark touring car. Heinrich Nussbaum took Jonathan Quicksilver, the Honorable Lama Lumpo Smythe-Finkel, and Howling Frog in the Edsel limo. Mrs. Starkley, Rat's English teacher, and her husband, Mr. Starkley, had a big motorcycle—Mrs. Starkley drove. K.E. Kelman, PH., and his mother, Lydia LaZonga Kelman, had a black van with the word PHANTOMOLOGIST lettered on each side. Phelps and Scott Feldman drove in their Gremlin with automatic transmission, cruise control, deluxe wheel covers, and vinyl roof. Osgood Sigerson had given the driver of each vehicle a sealed envelope.

"Have fun, everybody!" Osgood Sigerson had said, and belching exhaust fumes and borgelnuskies, we roared off into the night.

"Let's see what's in the envelope," Rat said. She tore open the envelope and read:

Greetings!
Tonight we catch the werewolf! Proceed to the Garden of Earthly Bliss Drive-in and Pizzeria. Pay your admission and drive in as though you were going to enjoy the films. Park anywhere. It is my belief that the werewolf will not be able to resist showing up, as the films tonight include *The Werewolf; The Werewolf of Poughkeepsie; I Was a*

Communist Werewolf; Werewolf Wars; and *Werewolf Stewardesses.* Sit in your cars and enjoy the show—but be on the lookout for the signal, which will consist of the lighting of a flare or torch by Dr. Sacker. When you see the signal, instantly come to the refreshment area, where I will give each of you a bouquet of wolfbane with which to confuse the lycanthrope. We will then spread out and chase the werewolf. At all costs prevent him from leaving the drive-in theater. Mr. K.E. Kelman and his mother, Lydia LaZonga Kelman, will be on hand with werewolf-capturing equipment. If we can direct the creature toward their van, which will be located at the center of the parking area, they assure me they can do the rest. Be vigilant! Be courageous! Be swift! Good Hunting!

—O. Sigerson, Esq.

"Wow!" Winston said.
"Definitely. Wow!" Rat said.
"Yeah. Wow." I said.

A horrible voice crackled through the loudspeaker. It was another recorded message from Wallace Nussbaum, coming over the car radio.

"Fools! You will never capture my creation! My werewolf is strong and clever and mean—and he can move so fast, it's as though he were in two places at once. I shall let you continue with your pathetic little exercise—just so you can see how really formidable my werewolf is. Don't blame me if you get a halyatchkie. You've been warned! Ha ha ha ha ha!"

"He's bluffing," Rat said.

"Right. He's bluffing," I said.

"Right," Winston said.

"Right."

"Right."

The Garden of Earthly Bliss Drive-in and Pizzeria, built by Louis Grotshkie, is generally agreed to be the finest outdoor movie theater in the world.

The giant screen is the size of two football fields. The projection system, specially made by Zeiss of Germany, has such superior powers of resolution that only brand-new prints of movies can be shown, because scratches and small imperfections on a film would appear as large as watermelons on the screen. The speakers, which are hooked over the windows of the cars of patrons, are in stereo pairs, and of the highest quality. There is a special noiseless gravel in the parking area, so that latecomers will not disturb with the sound of crunching tires.

Invisible bug-lights protect the patrons from mosquitoes. There is a full-scale amusement park for the children, complete with ferris wheel, pony rides, and an Olympic size swimming pool. Three European chefs supervise the preparation of pizza, which is baked and delivered directly to your car by an automated Japanese pizza chef robot, which runs on wheels and presents your pizza, piping hot, directly into your car window.

Full medical services, including a psychiatrist, are available should any patron become indisposed—and any baby born in the drive-in during the showing of a film receives a free pass, good weeknights, for life.

In addition to these regular services, the Garden of

Earthly Bliss Drive-in and Pizzeria offers occasional door prizes, including grand pianos, trips to Europe, mobile homes, and gold coins.

The visitor will note that the ticket kiosk and pizzeria/projection booth are built in the architectural style of the Mogoshoaia Palace, and the swimming pool is a replica of the Herculane Baths in the Cerna Valley in Romania. Before, after, or during the film, one is free to walk in a large formal garden built to resemble the Cishmigiu Garden in Bucharest.

The Garden of Earthly Bliss Drive-in and Pizzeria has received several awards from the Association of American Drive-in Movie Theaters and the International Brotherhood of Pizza Makers.

The fact is, I had never been to a drive-in movie. Neither had Rat. Neither had Winston. We drove out on Route 9R, looking for the Garden of Earthly Bliss Drive-in and Pizzeria. When we saw it, we flipped. It was great!

The place where you pay your admission looked like a castle or something. The screen was enormous. Band music was playing on all the loudspeakers, hundreds of them. The pizza smelled great. It was like a circus or a parade. Cars full of people were lined up for a mile, waiting to get into the drive-in. Once inside, the cars cruised around—the drivers trying to make up their minds about where to park. All this time, the band music was playing and colored lights were flashing on the great screen. There was this castle-type building in the middle of the place. Great big loudspeakers at the corners were blasting the band music, and this thing on wheels was running up and down in front of it.

The thing on wheels was a robot pizza chef. You could call your pizza order in by pressing a button and talking into one of the car speakers, and the robot would bring you your pizza, shove it through the car window, take your money, and give you your change. The card attached to the speaker said the Garden of Earthly Bliss Drive-in and Pizzeria could make *any* kind of pizza—just ask. What a great place!

The back part of the drive-in was like a carnival or

an amusement park. There were colored lights, rides—a ferris wheel, a roller coaster, ice cream stands, a swimming pool, and a big garden you could walk around in. And everywhere, band music.

I nearly forgot that we were there to catch a werewolf. The place itself was so spectacular, I would have been happy just to have come out there to watch five werewolf movies, maybe eat some pizza, and then go home.

We could see the Kelmans' van parked in the middle of everything, and we also could see Heinrich Nussbaum in the Edsel. None of the other cars were visible to us, but we assumed they were somewhere in the drive-in. Sigerson's instructions had been to sit in our car and enjoy the show. The show hadn't started yet, so we sat in our car and enjoyed the band music and the colored lights on the screen.

Ignatz the Igniter, a well-known Romanian pyromaniac, put fifteen or twenty books of matches in his pockets, checked his small bottle of gasoline, stuffed some automobile emergency flares into his shirt, wound several feet of slow-burning fuse around his ankle and covered it with his sock, filled his cigarette lighter, tucked several days' copies of the *Baconburg Free Press* under his arm, said a small prayer before a statue of Saint Barbara of Blint, kissed his mother, and went out for an evening's entertainment.

"Have a good time, son!" the mother of Ignatz the Igniter called.

```
                    ORDINARILY

                         I

                   DON'T   LIKE

                      DRIVE

                       IN

                     MOVIES

    THEY'RE DECADENT, AND APPEAL TO THE LOWEST ELEMENTS IN


                            SOCIETY

BUT

    THIS

          ONE'S

                   DIFFERENT      I SORT OF LIKE IT

                                  AND MY GURU PAID MY

                                  ADMISSION

SO I GET IN


                  FREE


                          *
```

Hark! Somewhere in the city, I hear a werewolf giving voice. Can it be that I am not alone? Somewhere one like me is growling. Humans are shrieking. It sounds like a party. I go to find the sound.

I, *Wallace Nussbaum, have done this thing. I alone have loosed upon the city my masterpiece of evil, my arch-awful impossible imp, my werewolf. How I love you, my sweet little werewolf! Wolf! Wolfy! Wolfaleh! Now I will take my rightful place among the Nussbaumic evil geniuses of history.*

Go, wolf-baby! Terrify! Destroy!

Osgood Sigerson, eat your heart out!

A car of foreign make pulls up to the ticket kiosk of the Garden of Earthly Bliss Drive-in and Pizzeria. It is a Wartburg, seldom seen in the West, but popular, because it's all you can get, in certain Soviet-bloc countries.

When the driver rolls down his window to pay his admission, the ticket-taker is struck by a whiff of Romanian "suicide-squad" salami mixed with the aroma of gasoline, paraffin, and other combustibles.

All types, high and low, enjoy the Garden of Earthly Bliss Drive-in and Pizzeria, and the Wartburg enters the great theater unhindered.

Dr. Ormond Sacker peered through a set of were-wolf-spotting glasses. "I don't see anything yet, Siger-son," he said. "That is, I don't see any sign of the werewolf. The behavior of some of the citizens of Ba-conburg, not to say the citizens themselves, I have been watching with immense disgust."

"Keep scanning for the werewolf, old chap," Os-good Sigerson, the world's greatest detective, said. "He's bound to turn up once the films start, if not sooner."

"How curious, Sigerson! Those people over there seem to be preparing a barbecue of some sort."

"Romanians from the village of Blint, no doubt," Osgood Sigerson said. "The security guards will be along in a moment to extinguish the fire and eject them."

"Amazing, Sigerson! You're absolutely right! The security guards are putting out the fire and making the people leave. Why do they do that, Sigerson?"

"Why do people from Blint set fires in drive-in movies?"

"Yes, Sigerson. Why do they do that?"

"All I can say is that I'm grateful that the strange proclivities of the former residents of Blint are none of my concern. I doubt whether they know themselves why they behave in that singular and annoying fash-ion. Since Blintians are law-abiding, apart from their penchant for arson in open-air theaters, I have had no occasion to deal with any of them. As you know, my ethnological interests are largely limited to peoples who specialize in crime. There is a village in Sikkim, for example, which produces nothing but high-grade felons. Nobody knows why."

"Lordey, this is boring," Dr. Ormond Sacker said. "I wish the werewolf would show up."

"Daddy, do you think we'll really catch the werewolf?"

"Shut up, son—the movie's starting."

"O.K., Sonny, let's go over it once more. Rope made of wolfbane."

"Check."

"Stainless steel handcuffs."

"Check."

"Stainless steel footcuffs."

"Check."

"Net."

"Check."

"Silver-headed clubs."

"Check."

"Garlic."

"Check."

"Mirrors."

"Check."

"Assorted religious artifacts, relics, and symbols."

"Check."

"Stereo recording of werewolves growling."

"Check."

"Bottle of synthetic werewolf fragrance."

"Check."

"Gas masks."

"Check."

"Bite-proof gloves."

"Check."

"Bite-proof boots."

"Check."

"Bite-proof trousers."

173

"Check."

"Extra-strong stainless steel cage, blessed by the Transylvanian monks."

"Check."

"Chain."

"Check."

"Muzzle."

"Check."

"Liver treats."

"Check."

"That's everything, Sonny. Now, let's just hope he shows up."

"Check."

Behind the wheel of his Wartburg, Ignatz the Igniter picks his teeth with a match. And waits. And
watches.

"Sigerson! I think I see something! It's moving be-tween the cars!"

"Just let me have those glasses, old fellow. Yes. Yes. I think our werewolf has arrived. Now, take this magnesium torch, and when I give you the word, run as fast as you can to the front of the theater, light the torch, and wave it about. That will be the signal for our friends to get out of their cars and dash like mad to the refreshment area, where I will be waiting with these bunches of wolfbane. Ah, this is the part I like. The game's afoot, Sacker, old thing. Now, be off with you!"

I run between the cars. I snarl and drool. Look! Up on the screen! Is it? It is! A wolfman like me! Oh, how beautiful! What a sad story! It seems so real! I feel! My senses reel! Never have I known such a thing. Can this be emotion, art-inspired? Does my wolfish heart feel sentiment, pity and terror? What shall I do? I am confused. Now, in this flickering movement of frame after frame, I stand transfixed, an unmoving picture. Oh, see! On the screen, my likeness is pursued. A posse impossibly persecutes my shadow. I must act. Never before have I hesitated, even for a moment.

What? A light! A flash! A torch! A flare! An idiot waving a torch! Something in my mind ignites! I have been thinking! Drat! That is something I never do! I scorn the images of light. I extinguish thought. I am myself again. I go to mangle the pizza kitchen.

The doctor waves his torch beneath and in front of the great screen.

Osgood Sigerson prepares to distribute bouquets of wolfbane to his helpers.

The snarkers, deputies of Osgood Sigerson, leave their cars and head for the refreshment area.

The werewolf is shaken loose from his moment of inaction, and moves off toward the refreshment area.

Wallace Nussbaum, sitting disguised in a nondescript Datsun, guesses what's what and starts out for the projection booth above the pizza kitchen.

Ignatz the Igniter thinks another firebug is about to steal his fun and bolts from his car, intent on making things hot.

On the screen, a giant werewolf cavorts and capers.

When we saw Dr. Ormond Sacker waving the torch, we headed straight for the refreshment area in the middle of the drive-in. Everybody arrived more or less at once. Osgood Sigerson handed each of us a bunch of wolfbane and told us to head for the edges of the parking area and work our way in toward the center, waving our wolfbane and hollering.

I felt something rush past me. For some reason, I pictured a dark wind. "A sudden storm coming up," I thought—but things were happening too fast to think clearly. Then there was a lot of noise and banging in the pizza kitchen—it sounded as if they were having some trouble with the equipment.

"Hurry to the edges of the parking area," Osgood Sigerson said. "I shall stay here with K.E. Kelman, PH., and Lydia LaZonga Kelman, and prepare to snatch the werewolf when he arrives, terrified and confused by all the noise you'll be making."

"Listen," Jonathan Quicksilver said, "about getting a werewolf terrified and confused . . . it isn't as easy as . . ."

"There's no time to exchange opinions now, Mr. Quicksilver," Osgood Sigerson said. "I respect the arts as much as anyone, and I have no doubt that you are a fine poet, but I must choose to accept the advice of professional werewolf experts."

"Well, I come from Transylvania originally, and . . ."

"Mr. Quicksilver, please! I must ask you to get busy now. We can talk after the werewolf is captured."

Quicksilver mumbled something under his breath and hurried off to the edge of the parking area to start waving his wolfbane and hollering. Rat, Winston, and I took up positions maybe fifty feet apart, and started closing in. We waved our wolfbane and shouted at the top of our lungs. The movie patrons, who were involved with the movie—it was the one in which a werewolf menaces Poughkeepsie—all told us to shut up.

They didn't have time to complain for long—something more distracting took their attention.

"FIRE!" someone shouted, and another voice in another part of the drive-in shouted "FIRE!" At first, I thought it had to do with Dr. Ormond Sacker, who was still waving his torch and being abused by people in the cars nearest to him. Then I smelled smoke and became aware of a flicker of flames at the base of the great screen.

The screen—or that part of the screen which was supposed to represent some architectural marvel in Europe—was on fire. The movie was still being projected onto the screen part of the screen, but flames were creeping up the sides, making a sort of flame-frame around the picture.

The reaction of the crowd was mixed. Some were screaming—some were cheering—and a group of people were singing what I later found out was a Romanian anthem of joy.

From his position near the pizza kitchen, Osgood Sigerson shouted, "Never mind the fire! There's no particular danger! Just keep waving the wolfbane and shouting and moving toward the center! Keep calm!"

Nobody was keeping calm. People were leaving the drive-in in droves. Others, apparently happy about the way things were turning out, stayed; still others seemed to be horrified and unable to tear themselves away from the events as they unfolded. Giant fire hoses were turned on. Mounted on tall poles throughout the drive-in, they were spinning like pinwheels, drenching everybody. The movie, now encircled by flames, was still showing. The Romanian choir was singing. We were shouting.

It's funny what you shout when you have to keep making a lot of noise. I found myself hollering *"Boo!"* over and over. Winston was sort of yodeling and shouting *"Yippee!"* like a cowboy. I heard Rat shouting *"James Dean, I love you,"* as she waved her bunch of wolfbane around.

We kept closing in on the center of the drive-in, where Sigerson and the Kelmans were waiting near the pizza kitchen and projection booth. There was a lot of smoke coming from the pizza kitchen, and a strong smell of burned pizza crust. That place was about to go up in flames too.

Something was careening crazily around the parking area. At first I thought it was the werewolf. Then I saw that it was the automated Japanese pizza chef robot. It had gone out of control. It was zooming up and down the aisles at high speed shooting hot pizzas out of its slot at car window height. Some of the Romanians got painful cheese burns.

As we converged on the center, we heard one another's shouts plainly. *"Oh, goody! We're going to catch the werewolf,"* I heard Scott Feldman shout. "What a shnerd!" I thought.

The film was still being projected onto the screen, surrounded by fire, only now there was an immense black shadow dancing and capering. It was a were-wolf—but not one on film. Something unmistakably horrible had gotten between the projector and the screen. It was the real thing! It must have been on the roof of a car, but with all the smoke and water from the fire hoses, and confusion, I couldn't see the werewolf, only its shadow. I was about to get scared by that, when something else scared me.

The voice of Wallace Nussbaum came over all the loudspeakers in the drive-in. I recognized it well enough—but even those who had never heard it stopped screaming, shouting, escaping, fire-fighting, and singing, and were terrified by the sound of it.

"Listen, fools! My werewolf cavorts.

I, Wallace Nussbaum, creator of the werewolf, and with whom the werewolf is in cahoots, cavort also.

The Mitsubishi Medium-Range Pizza Chef spits hot cheese at mine enemies.

Sigerson is a dumb-dumb.

Blintish Romanians sing their ancient song, un-aware that they are witnesses to the beginning of the end of everything.

The firehoses spin and drench and are of no use.

The film unreels and becomes reality.

Sing, you inhabitants of Blint.

Shout, you friends of Sigerson.

See, citizens of Baconburg, the end of the film comes soon.

The end of all you know and hold dear.
The end of culture—if you call this culture.
This is the vengeance of Nussbaum.
The beginning of my power.
I am your master—and you will be my slaves.
Hee hee hee hee hee!"

There was a noise as of scrambling and thumping, also shouting and gurgling. Somehow it was clear to all of us that what was happening was Nussbaum being shouldered aside, or the microphone grabbed away from him. The sounds of struggle lasted only a few seconds, and then another voice could be heard over the loudspeakers.

There was no mistaking whose voice this was. Looking at the screen to see that the silhouette was no longer there was just a matter of checking that which I already knew. What I was listening to—and what everybody else in the Garden of Earthly Bliss Drive-in and Pizzeria was listening to—was the voice of the werewolf—the Baconburg Horror.

There is no describing the quality of that voice. All I can say is that a thousand horrible images ran through my mind at once. I pictured claws scraping on a blackboard, breaking glass, a barrel of herring overturned, a McDonald's milkshake left overnight in August, rusty razor blades, industrial pollutants, Ronald Reagan singing Neapolitan ballads, bus fumes.

More horrible than the voice itself was what it was saying. It was too unbearable to listen to, but I had the sense that the werewolf was reciting a poem—a poem so monstrous, so vile, so evil that to listen to it for long would drive me insane.

"I think that I shall never see," the werewolf recited, *"a poem lovely as a tree."*

At that moment, K.E. Kelman, PH., and Lydia La-Zonga Kelman jumped the werewolf. It was lucky timing. I don't know how much more of the werewolf's reciting I could have endured.

There was a tremendous struggle. I didn't get to see any of it—it took place inside the projection booth. Later, I was told that the fancy equipment the Kelmans had brought was of no use. The special net, the handcuffs and footcuffs—none of it did any good. The werewolf snarled, knocked everybody sprawling, and bounded out of the projection booth, which was already on fire.

One good thing did happen. Sigerson managed to get handcuffs on Wallace Nussbaum, who was crawling around on the floor after having been shoved away from the microphone by the werewolf. Sigerson and Heinrich Nussbaum dragged Wallace out of the burning building.

"You're going to be thwarted this time," Heinrich said to his brother.

"That remains to be seen," Wallace Nussbaum said. "My werewolf is still free. By the way, how's Mommy?"

"She was fine the last time I saw her," Heinrich said.

"Look! There he goes! After him!" Osgood Sigerson shouted.

The werewolf was streaking away, darting among the remaining cars, the still smoldering pizzas, and the wreckage of what had once been the finest drive-in movie on earth.

THE MOST SPECTACULAR FIRE YET AT THE GARDEN OF
EARTHLY BLISS DRIVE-IN AND PIZZERIA . . . AND, . . . IS
THE BACONBURG HORROR AT AN END? DETAILS AT
ELEVEN.

It was Scott Feldman who caught the werewolf. The creature was making its way through the wreckage at high speed when it ran into Scott, who was waving his bunch of wolfbane and shouting "Oh, goody! We're going to catch the werewolf!" The werewolf paused, possibly to laugh, and Scott stuck his hand out and said, "Hello, my name is Scott Feldman." At the same time, he gazed at the creature with his well-known hypnotic stare. "I liked your poem," Scott said.

Louis Grotshkie, now a very old man, had been following the werewolf as best he could. He was convinced that he had at last caught up with Ignatz the Igniter, who had many times torched Grotshkie's great creation. Ignatz, in fact, was at that very moment sprinkling paraffin on the last gondola of the great ferris wheel, having already prepared the others.

Grotshkie, coming up behind the werewolf, raised his silver-headed walking stick and prepared to strike.

Ignatz raised his last waterproof kitchen match and prepared to strike.

"I liked your poem," Scott Feldman said to the werewolf.

At that moment, Louis Grotshkie brought down his walking stick with the utmost force.

At the same moment, Ignatz the Igniter lit the ferris wheel and pulled the lever setting it in motion.

At the same moment, the automated Japanese pizza chef, traveling at top speed and spewing fourteen-inch pizzas piping hot in every direction, struck the werewolf broadside, causing Grotshkie's blow to fall with a sickening thwack on a double-cheese-with-sausage-and-anchovies in midair.

Essentially unharmed, but slightly dazed by the impact of the robot, the werewolf was also distracted by the simultaneous splattering of the pizza and the sudden spectacle of the ferris wheel in flames.

At almost the same moment, but actually in the next one, K.E. Kelman, PH., and his mother, Lydia LaZonga Kelman, frustrated and inspired to superhuman vigor by their chagrin at the lycanthrope's earlier escape, fell upon him with stainless steel handcuffs, footcuffs, elbowcuffs, kneecuffs, and earmuffs, yards of wolfbane rope, extra-strong black electrical tape, and miracle glue.

In the next moment, or possibly the one after that, the werewolf was immobilized.

All of this was illuminated bright as day by the revolving flaming ferris wheel, visible all over the county.

By this time, the fire brigades had arrived. The streams of their hoses arched over everything. The Garden of Earthly Bliss Drive-in and Pizzeria was a battleground, soggy, smoldering, flickering, pizza-strewn.

"Next time, I build the whole thing out of asbestos," Louis Grotshkie said.

Rat was disgusted that it had been Scott Feldman who had, essentially, caught the werewolf. "We'll never hear the end of this," she said.

"What's more," Winston said, "he intends to take up snarking. We'll be seeing him here at the movies. He got permission from his father—can you beat that? Asking permission to sneak out of the house? Yick."

"When does Uncle Flipping get out of your sound-proof room?" I asked Rat.

"I think Osgood Sigerson is going to let him out soon," Rat said. "It's a week past the last full moon, and this time he just got slightly hairy—no howling or anything."

"So the marifesa Nussbaum was feeding him has just about worn off."

"So it seems," Rat said. "He still doesn't remember anything about being a werewolf."

"I read where they're deporting that orangutan—the one Nussbaum had working as a kitchen helper and doctoring Uncle Flipping's borgelnuskies at the Deadly Nightshade Diner—We Never Close."

"Well, the way I see it, it wasn't really his fault. Nussbaum hypnotizes the apes, and makes them do whatever he wants."

"Heinz—that is, Heinrich Nussbaum—is going back to Peru," Rat said.

189

"Yeah? He's a nice guy," Winston said.

"Not like his brother," I said.

"Yeah. That Wallace is evil. At least they've got him where he can't escape—the Château d'If."

"Yeah."

"Sigerson's going to leave town."

"Yeah. I heard."

"Well, anyway, Uncle Flipping will never be a werewolf again."

"No. That's true."

"Did you know that Jonathan Quicksilver is a manager at Ms. Doughnut now?"

"Is that so?"

"Oh, he's very serious about his work—hardly has time for poetry anymore."

"Hum."

The house lights started to go down. It was time for the movie to start. We settled down in our seats.

Then something amazing happened. Instead of the opening credits for *Utamaro, Painter of Women* there was the face of Wallace Nussbaum, filling up the whole screen. Nussbaum was laughing.

"Fools!" Nussbaum was saying, "I have escaped from the Château d'If. It was easy. I have spliced this film onto the beginning of every movie in every movie house in the world, and also in the middle of most television commercials—the only thing on TV anybody pays attention to. My purpose is to tell the world that I will strike again! I have plans! Horrible plans! And that fool Osgood Sigerson and his friends can do nothing to stop me! You have not heard the last of Wallace Nussbaum!"

Then the screen went dark. The movie house was silent, except for the sound of the three of us clapping and cheering.

F I N I S